A GUIDEBOOK TO CONTEMPORARY ARCHITECTURE IN MONTREAL

A GUIDEBOOK TO CONTEMPORARY ARCHITECTURE IN MONTREAL

NANCY DUNTON
HELEN MALKIN

WITH ESSAYS BY
GEORGES ADAMCZYK
RICARDO L. CASTRO

DOUGLAS & McINTYRE
VANCOUVER/TORONTO/BERKELEY

Douglas & McIntyre Ltd.
2323 Quebec Street, Suite 201
Vancouver, British Columbia
Canada V5T 4S7
www.douglas-mcintyre.com

Published simultaneously in French by Les Presses de l'Université de Montréal under the title *Guide de l'architecture contemporaine de Montréal* (ISBN 978-2-7606-2075-9)

Library and Archives Canada Cataloguing in Publication

Dunton, Nancy H.
 A guidebook to contemporary architecture in Montreal / Nancy Dunton, Helen Malkin ; with essays by Georges Adamczyk, Ricardo L. Castro.

Includes index.
ISBN 978-1-55365-346-2

 1. Architecture—Quebec (Province)—Montreal—20th century—Guidebooks. 2. Architecture—Quebec (Province)—Montreal—21st century—Guidebooks. 3. Montreal (Quebec)—Buildings, structures, etc.—Guidebooks. I. Malkin, Helen II. Adamczyk, Georges III. Castro, Ricardo L. IV. Title.

NA747.M65D85 2008
720.9714'2809045   C2007-904603-7

Texts: Nancy Dunton
Editing: Lynda Muir
Translation: Joshua Wolfe
Cartography: Eric Leinberger
Photography editing: Alain Laforest
Research: Christine Boucher
Drawing preparation: Solange Guaida

Book design: George Vaitkunas
Cover and full-page photographs: Alain Laforest

Printed and bound in China by C & C Offset Printing Co., Ltd.
Printed on acid-free paper

Distributed in the U.S. by Publishers Group West

Douglas & McIntyre gratefully acknowledges the financial support of the Canada Council for the Arts, the British Columbia Arts Council, the Province of British Columbia through the Book Publishing Tax Credit, and the Government of Canada through the Book Publishing Industry Development Program (BPIDP) for its publishing activities.

The authors gratefully acknowledge the financial support of the Canada Council in the preparation of the book.

Canada Council   Conseil des Arts
for the Arts   du Canada

Additional thanks go to the authors' families, friends and colleagues for their thoughtful comments and unflagging support.

CONTENTS

PREFACE

Why this book?

People who like to look at buildings like nothing better than being turned loose on a city with a good guidebook. After years of looking at contemporary architecture in other cities, it was frustrating not to be able to do so in one's own city. It was more frustrating still to not be able to hand a visitor that good guidebook and some metro tickets and send him or her out to see what Montreal had been building in the last twenty-five years.

There is good architecture in Montreal. There are flashes of more than good; there are moments that are effervescent and that's what makes Montreal so intriguing.

Why these buildings?

We selected buildings that we believe were well designed and possess an enduring quality, but equally, we asked ourselves whether the building had made a significant impact on its *quartier*. Had a project created new public space or contributed to civic life? Had it changed the way buildings were perceived in that neighbourhood? Did it use materials in an innovative way? Did it do a lot on a restrained budget? Does it transcend the time in which it was built?

Montreal is a city very vulnerable to economic cycles and to political events, so sometimes the reason why a building stands out is because of the time in which it was created. As Montrealers, we remember the recession of 1991–92 or we think of how audacious a gesture Usine C was – because nobody was building anything in the post-referendum deep freeze of 1995.

Sometimes the innovation is in the choice of *quartier* – for example, choosing to keep Johnson & Johnson in Hochelaga-Maisonneuve. Is the bold act the work of the architect or the decision of the client?

Sometimes what makes a building noteworthy – or visit-worthy – is that it asserts itself relative to those around it; and sometimes it's the obverse of the coin – a building makes itself known by quiet assurance.

Having a stock of interesting 19th-century buildings is one of Montreal's great assets; finding uses for them other than those for which they were intended is a skill that has been learned. Almost half the projects in this book about contemporary architecture intervene in existing buildings – they reuse, recycle, convert and add on. Some may now look a little dated or even timid by early 21st-century standards, but their value derives in part from how innovative they were in their time. The best, of course, have that ineffable quality of timelessness.

University buildings and cultural institutions are strongly represented as building types in this guidebook. Built as a way to inject money into the economy or – in the late 1990s – as the consequence of major individual donations to institutions, they have significantly changed the urban landscape of Montreal.

The Montreal housing type – the three-storey rowhouse with a common wall between it and its neighbours, and set back only by the width of an exterior staircase – is strong and ever-present in the city. Against this rich background, many of the most successful contemporary residential projects are those that declare themselves confidently as a type apart.

Hotels, restaurants, and retail interiors are not included in this book because, of necessity, they change so often. Since 1995, Design Montréal (originally Commerce Design Montréal) has promoted and published the best that the city has to offer in this, the most ephemeral type of design project.

Are there projects that should have been included but have not? Perhaps. While much effort has gone into rigorously assessing each project according to the criteria outlined above, the ultimate choice is subjective.

As well, of course, the limitations of time (a project had to be completed to be included) and space imposed themselves.

Why this time period?

The 1983 construction of Maison Alcan marked a shift in attitude, a shift towards a respect for the city and a connection to it that was for the most part absent in the 1970s. A greater public consciousness of Montreal as a whole in the 1980s – influenced by major architectural competitions and public consultations – affected the next generation of architects to graduate from the city's two schools of architecture. The projects in this book are, for the most part, the work of that generation and of those who taught them.

Who was this book written for?

Architects and designers, certainly, but more generally, people with an interest in and a curiosity about architecture. Implicit in the task that we set for ourselves – to write two hundred words about a given building – was the idea that the visitor standing on the sidewalk understood why a particular building was included.

The purpose of this guidebook is to allow the user to find buildings and places, and to discover something about them, to understand them in the context of Montreal's neighbourhoods. The projects selected represent what we would take visitors to see ourselves, what we would not want someone to miss.

Put the book in your pocket, get on the metro and go look at Montreal.

HOW TO USE THIS BOOK

Buildings and places in this book are all accessible by public transportation. Checking on hours and frequency of service of the bus and metro system is always advisable, at www.stm.ca. There are both public places and private houses in the guidebook, and every attempt has been made to be clear about access to buildings (websites for further information have been included), but respect for privacy has been, and we believe should remain, paramount.

Projects to see are grouped according to *quartier,* or neighbourhood – the names correspond to those on the city maps in sidewalk kiosks and in metro stations. A short text about each gives the visitor a sense of the neighbourhood, but there is, of course, much more to see and explore.

The sequence of *quartiers* within the book starts from the downtown core and moves in a spiral towards the east, then loops back to the west. The sequence of projects within each *quartier* typically starts from the building closest to a metro station.

Maps of *quartiers* are oriented towards nominal Montreal north – to a Montrealer, St. Laurent runs north-south and Sherbrooke east-west. (This perception is so ubiquitous that it actually appears on architectural drawings.) Representation of *quartiers* is based on historic and municipal definitions, although sometimes relaxed to better illustrate the context of the city. Metro stations are indicated by the metro symbol located at the most convenient entry point. As some stations have many entries, checking the metro system's neighbourhood map in the particular station may be useful.

The language of Montreal is French; most buildings are known only by their French names, so that is how they are titled in the book. When a building uses both an English and a French name, the English version is given. Street names, both in texts and on *quartier* maps, correspond to city maps and street signage, to make finding one's way about as easy as possible.

Images of projects are typically but not exclusively those which the architects themselves use to present their work, and in most cases show the project as it was at the time of completion. We are endlessly grateful to all the architects and photographers alike who responded to our requests for drawings and images.

Architects are identified by the name that the firm was known by at the time of project completion, as are clients. Indexes at the end of the guidebook are organized by building, by building type, and by architectural firm, to allow for cross-referencing.

MONTREAL ARCHITECTURES
GEORGES ADAMCZYK

For many years described as a city sitting on the border between America and Europe, Montreal is now a global city, in the only French-speaking province of North America. Buffeted by waves of immigration and municipal annexations, mergers and de-mergers, the limits of the city have shifted. However, its spectacular geography remains, little changed from the descriptions found in the accounts of the early explorers. First and foremost, Montreal is a majestic island in the St. Lawrence, about 500 square kilometres in area. Above the riverbanks looms Mount Royal, named by Jacques Cartier in 1535. Both a gateway to conquest and a commercial centre, the port spurred the city's growth from its founding in 1642.

At the beginning of the 20th century, the monumental architecture of banks and insurance companies rivalled with the industrial architecture of enormous grain elevators to transform a colonial city into a multi-coloured collection of lively streets and avenues. The island of Montreal now has 1.8 million inhabitants within a vast metropolitan area totalling 2.8 million. Even before setting out to see its contemporary architecture, visitors immediately sense that Montreal is a welcoming city. Walking through its neighbourhoods – each one so different and so lively in its own right – one sees the contrast between their vernacular brick rowhouses and the grey stone of the old city and the glass and steel that dominates the downtown core. The visitor quickly grasps the strong sense of place that Montrealers feel, which sets the city apart from others in North America. On the one hand, one is astonished by the excessiveness and the ambition of the built environment; on the other, charmed by the modesty and discretion of things.

How are these extremes combined in Montreal's contemporary architecture? The question can provide a measure for the poetry of expanses and materials that have influenced efforts by Montreal architects, as much as have the realities of uses and seasons. Let's turn first to history, to the drastic changes of the last few years and the aesthetic and social effects that have modified the horizon of architectural creation. This is the subject of this architectural guidebook, which presents with an inventive attitude the most significant and the most publicly accessible Montreal buildings.

The early 1980s marked an important moment in the history of urban development in Montreal. According to many observers and critics, this was the end of post-war modernism. The post-war period in Montreal saw the development of a new downtown, the glory years of international architecture, and the opening of the city to the entire world with the 1967 Universal Exposition, and with the exorbitant 1976 Olympic Games. It was also the time of Quebec's Quiet Revolution. From 1950 to 1980, the spaces and landscapes of Montreal were radically transformed. Undoubtedly, this period bears a similarity to the decades at the end of the 19th century and the start of the 20th which saw the dawn of modernity and the beginnings of an American identity for a city that had been French, then British. However, the post-war period was, more importantly, the swan song of modernism, which gave us unique buildings, rich in remarkable innovation. Today, unfortunately, we limit our appreciation of this time to a few architectural icons. Among these celebrated buildings, every self-respecting, cosmopolitan guidebook will mention Habitat 67, the U.S. Pavilion, Place Ville Marie and the underground city, Westmount Square, the Tour de la Bourse (Place Victoria) and Place Bonaventure.

The early 1980s was the onset of the post-modern period. French philosopher Luc Ferry's analysis of postmodernity suggests three trends: postmodernity as high modernism; postmodernity as revivalism – returning to tradition as opposed to modernism; and postmodernity as going beyond modernism, threatening to overtake reason, potentially to find the end of art. Contemporary architecture is primarily characterized by the first two trends, although architectural thinking has also been affected by the crisis in art. Montreal's principal Canadian rival, Toronto, chose high modernism. In contrast, Montreal did not seek to intensify its modernist heritage. Moreover, it was even less prone to dash in front of the lights shining on the hypermodernist stage to take part in the pathetic deconstructions with which it is cluttered. Instead, Montreal can be identified with the second trend. The city fell back on a vernacular tradition, the architecture of its past, and rejected a modern architecture that had itself become the academic tradition.

This attitude of resistance did not reject creativity but it did oppose the violent aspects of urban development that tended to destroy everything in the name of progress. Abandoning the search for universal values prom-ised by modernism, society in general – and architectural production in particular – was motivated by a dualistic cultural process of recognition and appropriation. Consequently, the preservation and reuse of built heritage gained a momentum that was only equalled by that of popular enthusiasm for the increase of Quebec's autonomy within Canada. Maison Alcan, designed in 1983 by Arcop, is the best symbol of this turnaround. These architects, renowned for the brutalist aesthetic of their projects, shifted architectural innovation toward a dialogue between the contemporary value of new construction and the heritage value of existing buildings on redevelopment sites. Going beyond the categorical opposition that soci-ologist Manuel Castells noted between "renovation by bulldozer" and "conservation-recycling," henceforth it was more a matter of a culturalist approach to urban planning and a contextual approach to architecture in Montreal.

Reshaping the urban form – and especially the reconfiguration of accom-panying public spaces – is seen by many observers as the concrete beginnings of the re-conquest of the city by its residents. This is the best place from which to appreciate the renewal of architecture. It is also a good way for visitors to make contact with Montreal's contemporary designers.

During the 1970s, the issue of how to redevelop surplus port properties arose, with attempts to impose an imperious urban development that lacked any consideration for the historic values and public interest of this unique site. Following an exemplary public consultation and an international ideas competition, in 1991 architects Cardinal Hardy, with Peter Rose and Jodoin Lamarre Pratte et Associés proposed a development plan for this large site. The Old Port site was divided into two design areas: on the east, the Bonsecours Basin sector, on the west, the Locks sector. Inarguably, here history informs the composition of architecture and landscape, whether pre-existing or newly created. The development plan becomes an interpretive strategy. The peak years of harbour use – 1930 to 1960 – were the main reference, although there are also allusions to previous centuries. As visitors move through the site, they can easily identify traces of the first broad wharves along de la Commune St. Whereas the East Sector is a place where plantings and structures formally display and analogously evoke the image of an active port, the West Sector offers a large worksite of industrial archaeology open to the public. Here, the composition is more narrative and provides visual emphasis to the entrance to the Lachine Canal and the restored locks. At the foot of the Silo No. 5 complex stands the Maison des Éclusiers, a well-designed, modest building that skilfully develops an architectonic lexicon inspired by industrial artefacts.

The Montreal Science Centre opened in 2000 on the King Edward Pier. Developed by the consortium of architects Gauthier Daoust Lestage/ Faucher Aubertin Brodeur Gauthier, this project follows the interpretive strategy established by the Old Port development plan. With great simplicity, a parallel pair of large hangars was recycled, one into the Centre, the other primarily for parking. Applying in almost subliminal fashion the principle that a building is a strict composition of its program, structure and envelope, the architects applied an extremely formalist, almost minimalist, rigour to these buildings. As a result, the gigantic scale of the project is forgotten. On the inside, the structure is perceptible, easily comprehended; thus, a visit to the Centre offers both a lesson in techniques and an architectural pleasure. Another remarkable building links the Old Port to Old Montreal: the Musée de la Pointe-à-Callière, especially the *Éperon*, or spur, designed by Dan Hanganu in collaboration with Provencher Roy and constructed in 1993. The solid presence of this building and its slender tower create a metaphor for ongoing history. The cylindrical form evokes the grain elevators; its masonry recalls the typical building material of the old city; its modern lines are supported by a classical composition. All of this melds the past and the future with a kind of found innocence – a rare quality in architecture.

The Cité Multimédia and the Quartier international de Montréal are two major urban redevelopment projects that have greatly contributed to the emphasis on a return to sources in the historic city and its *faubourgs,* the original suburbs. The transformation of the Faubourg des Récollets into the Cité Multimédia furthers the debate on the contemporary city and the world of research and experimentation in new technologies. The architecture of cables and wireless networks has diffused through the architecture of the city. As a unit, this old abandoned industrial district was recycled to house cutting-edge software companies. However, this is far from the temples of high tech. The tight network of city streets, the narrow blocks with traverse lots sufficient to accommodate several projects, completed and under construction; all have appropriated the language and appearance of Montreal buildings of the industrial age.

Among the many projects, two stand out for the quality of their execution. The first was completed in 1998 and received the Grand Prix d'Excellence of the Ordre des architectes du Québec. Architects Annie Lebel, Geneviève l'Heureux and Stéphane Pratte of Atelier in situ recycled the Weir Marine Outfitters Building for Discreet Logic and Behaviour Entertainment. The second is a new building, Cité Multimédia, phase 8, designed by architects Menkès Shooner Dagenais/Dupuis LeTourneux in 2001. Marking the entrance to downtown, it plays in two scales: that of the metropolis and that of the *quartier.*

The master plan created by the architectural consortium of Gauthier Daoust Lestage and Provencher Roy for the Quartier international de

Montréal is a highly sophisticated urban project. The plan shaped all elements – lighting, street furniture, public art, street design – to ensure a strong sense of identity for the district. The project is very contemporary in appearance. In its public spaces it offers an image likely to respond to the demands of a cosmopolitan clientele, one that travels frequently and whose tastes are attuned to globalized sensibilities with regard to space and forms. It is easy to fall for the clichés of supermodernity and create sophisticated non-places such as airports, convention centres, shopping malls, hotels and office buildings. They can be found all over the world and are often designed by the same major international architectural firms. But Montreal is not Singapore, nor Dubai. The location of the Quartier international, between the downtown core and Old Montreal, called for a local, referential approach to the architectural context; the result successfully meets the challenge.

In addition to Place Bonaventure and the Tour de la Bourse, which define the western boundary of the Quartier international de Montréal, three projects contribute to its distinctive identity. The first of these was completed in 1991: the Centre de commerce mondial linked a number of existing buildings by adding a public corridor, the Ruelle des Fortifications, interiorized under a grand glass structure. All the period façades were conserved, and the additional buildings of the complex were inspired by the architecture of St. Jacques St., for many years Montreal's financial and banking artery. Led by architects Arcop Associés and Provencher Roy, this hybrid project has become the contact point between the Quartier international and Old Montreal.

The second, the design of the expansion to the Palais des congrès, was the result of a controversial competition won by an architectural consortium of Tétrault Parent Languedoc / Saia Barbarese Topouzanov / Aedifica with Hal Ingberg. The architects provided a strong concept, much of which is based on the tectonic qualities of the construction, and particularly, on the use of coloured glass for the new façade on Place Riopelle. In addition to integrating the 1983 convention centre building by Victor Prus, which rises above the Ville-Marie expressway trench, the new project encompasses historic buildings on St. Antoine. Moreover, it completes the underground network linking Place Bonaventure and Place des Arts. The project also provides vast east-west and – more importantly – north-south urban corridors. These corridors improve the link between Old Montreal and the rest of the city.

The third project, the Centre CDP Capital, is by architects Gauthier Daoust Lestage and Faucher Aubertin Brodeur Gauthier, the consortium also responsible for the Montreal Science Centre. The headquarters of the Caisse de dépôt et placement du Québec, this 2003 building reconnects with the modernist theme of the curtain-wall via its innovative building envelope. The structure occupies the entire block between McGill, St. Antoine, Place Riopelle and Viger. A long glazed *passerelle* links Place Riopelle to McGill St. It connects the rear façade of existing buildings on St. Antoine St. with the new building on Viger. While this strategy is reminiscent of the Ruelle des Fortifications component of the Centre de commerce mondial de Montréal and Calatrava's BCE Galleria in Toronto, its intentions go further. An emphasis on bioclimatic functionality has led to high energy performance in the complex. In keeping with their approach, the architects provide a composition that is literal, practical and economic in appearance, while efficient and elegant in terms of technical decisions.

Horizontality dominates in each of these projects. The permeability of places and their spatial linkage promote a reshaping of the urban form and the creation of innovative public spaces. No skyscrapers, no acrobatics, and a complete absence of extravagance. Based on a concern for architecture's concrete qualities, the recognition of uses and their creative diversity, Montreal architecture is now well connected to the "Montrealness" described and defended by architect-critic-artist Melvin Charney.

The first experience of contemporary Montreal architecture must, necessarily, be followed by impressions of performance spaces. A city where language and speech are highly important, Canada and Quebec's cultural metropolis, Montreal is above all the artistic capital of Quebec. The Conseil des Arts de Montréal, founded in 1956, is the oldest arts council in Canada. In the 1980s, several international art events were born here, including the Festival International de Jazz de Montréal, the Festival de Théâtre des Amériques (now the Festival TransAmériques), the Festival International de Nouvelle Danse, and the Cent Jours d'Art Contemporain (now the Biennale de Montréal). In addition, the city hosts the "Just for Laughs" Comedy Festival, the FrancoFolies, the World Film Festival, the Festival du Nouveau Cinéma, the Festival International du Film sur l'Art. Many of these events offer activities in public spaces, creating a succession of temporary installations. The main purpose of the projected Quartier des Spectacles around Place des Arts is to bring the ideas of event and of the temporary – that ephemeral quality – to urban design. And not to be forgotten, the 1980s was also the time when street performers introduced the entire world to the Cirque du Soleil. Each of its new creations is presented under a big-top tent in the Old Port.

Montreal's insistence on artistic vitality is due to a desire to encourage visitors to explore the new venues for artistic productions. The architects of most of these small performance halls were able to show restraint in expression – but precision and vigour in the execution – while meeting the needs of the work and the audience. Théâtre du Rideau Vert, Théâtre d'Aujourd'hui, Cinémathèque Québécoise, and Usine C by architects Saucier + Perrotte; Espace Go, by FABG; Espace Chorégraphique Jean-Pierre Perreault by architect Pierre Thibault – each is astonishing in the simple and restrained way it distances itself from the spectacular exhibitionism so fashionable today. Other examples of cultural architecture's resistance to the globalizing stampede which should be visited are the Grande Bibliothèque and the Canadian Centre for Architecture. On a much larger scale than the performance spaces mentioned above, these two designs respond to their expressive mission with assurance and integrity. They are both part of Quebec's cultural landscape, to be sure, but each is undeniably of its location, one in the east, one in the west. Both convey a justifiable mistrust in the flights of monumentalism that claim to be inspired by democracy.

In an attempt to conclude this introduction which is still too short to do justice to the critical exciting work of the authors, it occurs to me that we can take inspiration from Umberto Eco. We can approach Montreal as an open architectural work. It is also a city that celebrates minorities, a kind of minority city. Consequently, it is often in a minor key that architecture is expressed, although this does not exclude major results. Two minor projects – Jacques Rousseau's Maison Coloniale (1990) and the Jardin des Premières-Nations pavilion, designed by Gilles Saucier and André Perrotte (2001) – are noteworthy for their meaningful intensity; they carry us away with subtle allegories on humanity's efforts to build and inhabit a land that must also be preserved.

Parc du Mont-Royal

Redpath-Crescent

Cedar

des Pins

du Docteur-Penfield

Côte-des-Neiges

Simpson

Redpath

du Musée

de la Montagne

Drummond

Stanley

McTavish

Lincoln

Sherbrooke

Jean-Noël Desmarais Pavilion, Montreal Museum of Fine Arts

Maison Alcan

Métro McGill

de Maisonneuve

Métro Peel

Métro Guy-Concordia

Sainte-Catherine

Metcalfe

Mansfield

McGill College

University

du Fort

Saint-Marc

Saint-Mathieu

EV Building, Concordia University

Peel

Tupper

Baile

Mackay

Bishop

Crescent

René-Lévesque

Square Dorchester

Seymour

Canadian Centre for Architecture

Guy

CCA Garden

1250 Boulevard René-Lévesque

Place du Canada

de la Gauche

Autoroute Ville-Marie

Métro Bonaventure

Métro Bonaventure

Métro Georges-Vanier

Métro Lucien-Lallier

Saint-Antoine

Saint-Jacques

0   200 metres
2 minutes to walk

Notre-Dame

DOWNTOWN

Montrealers not only work in the downtown core – they live, play and shop there. To go downtown invariably means to walk along Ste. Catherine, a street first fashionable in the 1890s when department stores moved up the hill from Square Victoria. In 1860, the newly wealthy had begun to flee the original downtown in Old Montreal to build elegant homes to the north of Sherbrooke. The city's financial centre, however, remained on St. Jacques in Old Montreal until Place Ville Marie was built in 1962.

Construction of the metro in 1966 changed the nature of downtown. Underground connections linked buildings not only to the subway system but also to one another; developers started to look for sites contiguous to metro stations. Construction of Place des Arts and Complexe Desjardins – both "hard-wired" to the metro – succeeded in moving the core of downtown slightly to the east.

A 1980s proposal to widen McGill College, the avenue leading north from Place Ville Marie to Sherbrooke, instigated public consultations that were as much about corporate presence in the downtown as they were about street width and setbacks. The granite and glass towers from that period remain a disappointment.

Much of 1990s downtown construction was institutional – universities, museums and theatres – and in part government-funded. By 2000, an upswing in the economy meant a rush to convert existing buildings into condominiums and to erect new ones, reinforcing the mixed residential and commercial character of Montreal's downtown.

MAISON ALCAN

The integration of new construction with restored or renovated buildings to create Alcan's world headquarters on Sherbrooke was an innovation at the beginning of the 1980s. It marked a turning point in corporate Montreal's attitude towards constructing offices, demonstrating that a tall building is not the only answer to corporate presence in the city. In this case, a new eight-storey pavilion was built behind three 19th-century greystone houses and a 1920s hotel, which were converted into offices; the whole is linked by a glazed atrium. The Davis Building is clad in a beautifully-detailed champagne-coloured aluminum curtain wall which is aging effortlessly.

Maison Alcan shares the block to the south with the former Salvation Army Citadel and office building linked to it, creating an urban park that reflects partner-in-charge Ray Affleck's views on the importance of the relationship of inside to outside, of being able to move freely through the building.

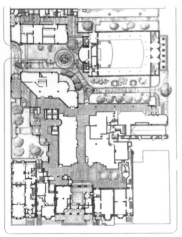

Sherbrooke

Architects	**Arcop Associates**
Client	**Alcan Aluminium Ltd.**
Completed	**1983**
Address	**1188 Rue Sherbrooke Ouest**
Métro	**Peel**
Access	**atrium open weekdays during office hours**

JEAN-NOËL DESMARAIS PAVILION, MONTREAL MUSEUM OF FINE ARTS

The new pavilion for the Montreal Museum of Fine Arts, sited directly opposite the original 1912 Edward & W.S. Maxwell building, was controversial from the very beginning of the project. The original scheme, calling for the demolition of the New Sherbrooke apartment building, excited opposition from many Montrealers and generated public consultations.

The outcome was the decision to retain the shell of the apartment building for museum offices, which added to the list of constraints that the difficult and highly visible site imposed. Safdie's solution was a series of three volumes connected by bridges – an entry pavilion, the refitted New Sherbrooke and a pavilion to the south of the alley running from Bishop to Crescent. The monumentality of the entry, a massive masonry arch opening to an atrium, may have been a deliberate counterpoint to the streetscape, but has still never truly looked as if it belonged.

A tunnel below Sherbrooke connects the 1991 construction to the much-modified and expanded 1912 building. A succession of Montreal architects have worked on this building over the years. The original addition was by Arcop in the 1970s; more recent interventions include an elegant escalator/elevator insertion by Provencher Roy in 1999.

Architects	**Moshe Safdie / Desnoyers Mercure et Associés / Lemay Leclerc**
Client	**Montreal Museum of Fine Arts**
Completed	**1991**
Address	**1380 Rue Sherbrooke Ouest**
Métro	**Guy-Concordia**
Access	**museum open Tuesday to Sunday / www.mmfa.qc.ca**

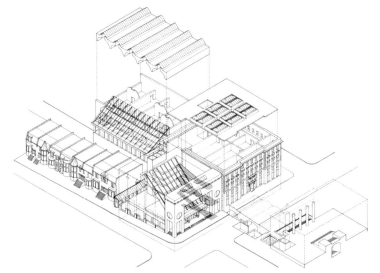

CANADIAN CENTRE FOR ARCHITECTURE

At the same time as it fulfils its mandate as a research centre and museum promoting the art and history of architecture, the Canadian Centre for Architecture also establishes its place clearly as a Montreal building. Its scale and volume reflect both the residential character of its Shaughnessy Village neighbourhood and the institutional nature of the convents within a stone's throw on René-Lévesque.

The CCA was built around the existing 1874 Shaughnessy House; the two wings of the new construction house the study centre to the east and the theatre to the west; exhibition galleries are in the central core. The collection of prints, drawings, photographs, books and other objects is stored in two floors of vaults below grade. The symmetry of the construction is generated by the party wall between the two halves of the original semi-detached house, visible on the north entry façade as a deftly incised expansion joint.

The choice of limestone – the stone out of which much of Montreal is built – for the exterior walls, and Quebec granite, aluminum and maple for the interior was a deliberate decision that reflects the CCA's sense of place. Designed to last a hundred years, the construction of the building demonstrates a commitment to quality that is *sans pareil*.

Architects	**Peter Rose**
Consulting architect	**Phyllis Lambert**
Associate architect	**Erol Argun**
Client	**Canadian Centre for Architecture**
Completed	**1989**
Address	**1920 Rue Baile**
Métro	**Guy-Concordia**
Access	**museum open Wednesday to Sunday / www.cca.qc.ca**

CCA GARDEN

The demolition in the mid-20th century of the Victorian-era houses on the south side of René-Lévesque and the construction of access ramps to the Ville-Marie expressway created a curious vestigial piece of land directly across the street from the Canadian Centre for Architecture. Charney's 1988 competition-winning design makes full use of the spectacular position of the land at the edge of the escarpment. It uses the rich history of the area to create layers and meaning in every aspect of the garden, making it a place of discovery.

The arcade evokes the demolished houses and mirrors the 1874 Shaughnessy House; the sculpture court is lined with allegorical columns that refer to the history of architecture and draw the eye to the cityscape below the belvedere. Low walls are sited on the cadastral lines that determined Montreal's street grid.

An apple orchard on the eastern edge of the garden recalls the original use of this part of the city – all the vegetation is deliberately indigenous. The CCA Garden serves as a place of reflection and respite in an area of the city that desperately lacked breathing space.

Architects **Melvin Charney**
Landscape architects **Gerrard and Mackers**
Client **Canadian Centre for Architecture**
Completed **1989**
Address **Boul. René-Lévesque between du Fort and Saint-Marc**
Métro **Guy-Concordia**
Access **public / www.cca.qc.ca**

EV BUILDING, CONCORDIA UNIVERSITY

Concordia University's downtown campus is made of concrete streets and sidewalks; there is little open land, and sites available for new construction are constrained. The architects' solution for a new building to house Engineering/Computer Science and Visual Arts was what they describe as "stacked academic neighbourhoods." The complex comprises two pavilions connected horizontally by intersecting circulation systems. Vertically, each pavilion has a series of stacked atria with circular stairs linking different floors and terraces.

For a university building, it has a very corporate look, with its projecting canopies at roof level and banded curtain wall. (The exception is the photographic floral mural by Nicolas Baier splashed over the east façade.) Much has been made of the transparency at the concourse level, but the three-storey interior space it reveals at the main entry corner at Guy and Ste. Catherine is rather unresolved. By contrast, the connections to below grade are some of the most interesting parts of the building: the escalator that leads to the metro station slices dramatically down into the underground level beside an illuminated wall.

Architects	**Kuwabara Payne McKenna Blumberg / Fichten Soiferman et Associés**
Client	**Concordia University**
Completed	**2005**
Address	**1515 Rue Sainte-Catherine Ouest**
Métro	**Guy-Concordia**
Access	**university hours**

1250 BOULEVARD RENÉ-LÉVESQUE

There were many tall buildings built in Montreal's downtown core in the 1980s, but the only one that comes close to the quality of its predecessors from the 1960s – Place Ville Marie, CIBC and Westmount Square – is 1250 René-Lévesque (known to Montrealers as the IBM Building for its original anchor tenant). Viewed from a distance, it is a classic skyscraper with a base, shaft and the grand gesture of a giant beak-like cap reaching towards the river. A closer view reveals the curve of the principal façade and the cluster of pavilions around the base. The volumes are deliberately complex. Black granite, white granite, aluminum and glass are played against one another.

Sitting strategically just west of Square Dorchester and north of Windsor Station, the building has volumetrically well-developed relationships with its neighbours. The changes of level and scale make the plaza more interesting than most, despite the chilly black granite pergola on Stanley.

Architects	**Kohn Pedersen Fox / Larose Petrucci et Associés**
Client	**IBM Canada / La Société immobilière Marathon, Limitée**
Completed	**1993**
Address	**1250 Boul. René-Lévesque Ouest**
Métro	**Bonaventure**
Access	**atrium open weekdays during office hours**

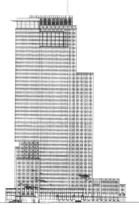

Parc du Mont-Royal

des Pins

McGill University and Génome Québec Innovation Centre

Trottier Building

Prince-Arthur

Aylmer

Nahum Gelber Law Library

Tomlinson Square

M.H. Wong Chemical Engineering Building

Docteur-Penfield

Lorne

Aylmer

Milton

Stanley

Peel

McTavish

University

Schulich School of Music

Sherbrooke

Victoria

McCord Museum of Canadian History

Président-Kennedy

Métro McGill

Metcalfe

Mansfield

de Maisonneuve

Métro Peel

McGill College

Union

0   100 metres

1 minute to walk

McGILL UNIVERSITY

The main campus of McGill University is the site of James McGill's country estate left in 1813 as a legacy, along with £10,000, to establish the university. Philanthropists such as Sir William Macdonald underwrote the construction of much of the campus in the latter half of the 19th century – a period of expansion that continued until the 1920s. Post-1945 construction started to encroach on the green space and produced mixed results architecturally as the university built rapidly to accommodate the baby boom.

Like the three other Montreal universities, McGill has been on a building spree since the late 1990s with a half-dozen different new buildings inserted into the campus. The McGill neighbourhood is actually much larger than the main campus, having spread into the late Victorian mansions on the slopes of the mountain.

M.H. WONG CHEMICAL ENGINEERING BUILDING

The 1998 M.H. Wong Building was the first new construction on the McGill University campus in twenty years. Inserted into the northeast corner of the downtown campus, it encompasses the 1948 Foster Cyclotron Building and houses departments that were bursting out of the McConnell Engineering Building to the south.

The structure has two distinct faces: a glass and aluminum curtain wall on Docteur-Penfield, the city side, and a limestone façade on the campus side. Materials allude to the 19th-century buildings that dominate the campus; the two-storey metallurgical foundry is clad in lead-covered copper. The north façade, the most interesting volumetrically, is now obscured in part by the 2003 construction of the adjacent Genome Building.

The interior of the Wong Building, with its four-storey-high hall, strongly declares its engineering vocation. Materials are industrial, the scale is large, and the main stairway marches resolutely upwards beside the stone wall of the existing Cyclotron Building. Laboratories and office spaces are reached via brightly-lit corridors, in contrast to the darkness of the main entry hall.

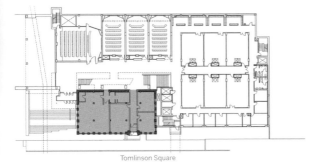

Tomlinson Square

Architects **Jodoin Lamarre Pratte et Associés / Marosi + Troy**
Client **McGill University**
Completed **1998**
Address **3610 Rue University, enter via Milton**
Métro **McGill**
Access **university hours**

McGILL UNIVERSITY AND GÉNOME QUÉBEC INNOVATION CENTRE

"Legible" is the word that best describes the Genome Building, as it is known. One sees immediately how to move through the building – all the more remarkable given that it has two fronts, one on the west towards Docteur-Penfield and one on the east towards Tomlinson Square.

Offices for researchers are on the more public west façade. Each office is articulated and canted slightly towards Mount Royal, protected by a screen of metal grid against the sun. Laboratories are on the sombre east façade on the campus side, behind a more formal curtain wall that sits on a limestone base. The two functions of the building are knit together by a three-storey vertical atrium, with circulation through it and conference rooms looking onto it. Common areas provide places for both formal and informal meetings.

Architects	**Kuwabara Payne McKenna Blumberg / Fichten Soiferman et Associés**
Client	**McGill University**
Completed	**2003**
Address	**740 Av. du Docteur-Penfield, enter via Milton**
Métro	**McGill**
Access	**interior lobbies only – university hours**

TOMLINSON SQUARE

Inserted into the already dense fabric of the northeast corner of McGill's downtown campus, Tomlinson Square redefines this interstitial space. Built on a former service road that terminated at the 1908 Strathcona Anatomy and Dentistry Building, this succession of promenade, courtyards and stairways makes walking up the steep slope a rewarding act. Materials change at different levels, and the fountain becomes a destination; once there, the visitor is surprised by an intriguing slice of the city revealed towards the south.

The relationship between this public space and the surrounding structures is made stronger by two projects that date to almost the same time – the Genome (2003) and Trottier (2004) buildings. The earlier M.H. Wong Building from 1998 and the 1978 Rutherford Building don't sit quite as comfortably at the southern edge.

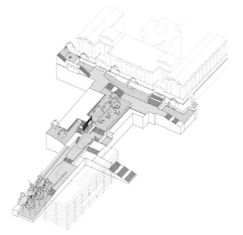

Architects **Marosi + Troy / Jodoin Lamarre Pratte et Associés**
Consultants **Schème**
Client **McGill University**
Completed **2004**
Address **McGill University Campus, enter via Milton**
Métro **McGill**
Access **public**

TROTTIER BUILDING

In contrast to the cool sobriety of the Genome Building, the Trottier is characterized by an openness and a sense of being an extension of the landscape of Tomlinson Square. Like the Genome and Wong buildings, the Trottier Building is double-sided – it addresses the interior, campus space on the west and University on the east. The restrained stone-and-glass east façade has been skilfully added to the streetscape.

The planning is open and obvious, and movement through the building is logical and well-organized. The lower three floors are classrooms for Electrical Engineering and IT programmes, while the upper three floors house laboratories and work spaces.

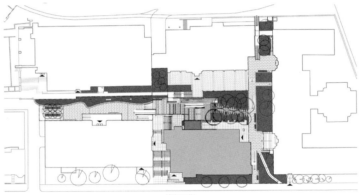

University

Architects	**Marosi + Troy / Jodoin Lamarre Pratte et Associés**
Client	**McGill University**
Completed	**2004**
Address	**3630 Rue University**
Métro	**McGill**
Access	**university hours**

NAHUM GELBER LAW LIBRARY

Old Chancellor Day Hall, the 1892 Square Mile mansion by the American architect Bruce Price, is the core of a cluster of buildings that are home to McGill's Faculty of Law. The Nahum Gelber Library was added at right angles to Chancellor Day Hall, sited so as to create an entry courtyard which sets up an opposition to the urban language of the surrounding area.

The choice of materials – brown brick and red stone – reflects the Victorian houses on Peel, while the rectangular box volume has more to do with the library's function as container. The two-storey triangular window, clearly intended to echo the surrounding turrets, is an example of the wit that infuses all of Hanganu's buildings.

The relationship of inside to outside and the presence of natural light play an important role; as one enters the lobby, a two-storey-high window reveals a small garden carved into the face of the hill behind the building, and slit-like windows mark the locations of study carrels.

Playfulness with industrial materials – another Hanganu trademark – is evident throughout: a purple metal spiral stair curves upward to the reference area, where the reading room occupies the top floors, and floor grates are used on the entrance doors.

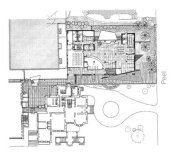

Architects	**Dan S. Hanganu**
Client	**McGill University**
Completed	**1998**
Address	**3660 Rue Peel**
Métro	**McGill**
Access	**interior – library lobby only, library hours**

McGill UNIVERSITY

McCORD MUSEUM OF CANADIAN HISTORY

The McCord Museum has been housed in the former McGill Student Union since 1967 when the original 1906 Percy Nobbs building was gutted to accommodate David Ross McCord's extensive collection of artefacts of Canadian history.

In the late 1980s, a donation by the J.W. McConnell Foundation finally allowed the museum to build both exhibition space and climate-controlled storage. The programme included both renovation of the existing building and new construction that tripled the existing floor area by extending the building to the south. Clad in the same limestone as the original building, the extension speaks a language that is both respectful and elegant in its own right. The glazed link and a lightwell onto an interior courtyard to the east mark the passage from old to new construction; large galleries are housed in the addition, smaller galleries for the permanent collections, main entrance, boutique and café in the original structure. A carefully controlled palette of materials including slate is used consistently through the building.

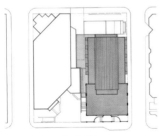

Sherbrooke

Architects	**Jodoin Lamarre Pratte et Associés / LeMoyne Lapointe Magne**
Client	**McCord Museum of Canadian History**
Completed	**1991**
Address	**696 Rue Sherbrooke Ouest**
Métro	**McGill**
Access	**Tuesday to Sunday, Mondays in summer / www.musee-mccord.qc.ca**

SCHULICH SCHOOL OF MUSIC

The Schulich School of Music is a building that demands attention, sitting as it does where Sherbrooke curves slightly at the corner of Aylmer. Juxtaposed and linked to the 1899 Strathcona Hall building (originally Royal Victoria College) housing McGill's Faculty of Music, it anchors the southeast corner of the McGill campus. The original programme to house the music library was expanded to include a five-storey-high scoring stage, rehearsal spaces, a 200-seat recital hall, and an opera studio. On a relatively narrow site, fitting in all of this meant assembling a three-dimensional puzzle, then literally digging three storeys down into the rock of Mount Royal to make room for it.

There is a controlled complexity to the building's façades – on the eastern side, the limestone base and horizontal bands of grey zinc represent the "geological" presence of the massive sound studio, and library, office and rehearsal spaces above it. By contrast, the western façade is vertical rusting steel topped by black glass, fragmented by contrasting slits.

The three-storey library sits behind a glazed slot on the front façade, creating a window-on-the-world place to sit and work. Wonderful small spaces and junctions happen all through the building, an attitude that characterises Saucier + Perrotte's work.

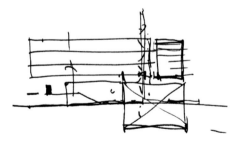

Architects	**Saucier + Perrotte / Menkès Shooner Dagenais LeTourneux**
Client	**McGill University**
Completed	**2005**
Address	**555 Rue Sherbrooke Ouest**
Métro	**McGill**
Access	**via adjacent Strathcona Building, university hours**

McGILL UNIVERSITY

53

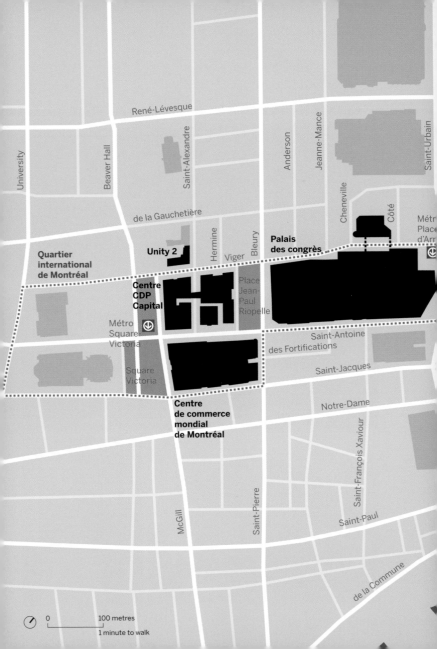

René-Lévesque

University

Beaver Hall

Saint-Alexandre

Anderson

Jeanne-Mance

Saint-Urbain

Cheneville

Côté

de la Gauchetière

Hermine

Viger

Bleury

Palais des congrès

Métro Place d'Arr

Unity 2

Quartier international de Montréal

Centre CDP Capital

Place Jean-Paul Riopelle

Métro Square Victoria

Saint-Antoine

des Fortifications

Saint-Jacques

Square Victoria

Centre de commerce mondial de Montréal

Notre-Dame

Saint-François Xaviour

McGill

Saint-Pierre

Saint-Paul

de la Commune

0   100 metres

1 minute to walk

QUARTIER INTERNATIONAL DE MONTRÉAL

The Quartier international de Montréal is a new "made-to-measure" *quartier*, a 27-hectare neighbourhood created by the owners of the buildings that sit within its borders, in a private-public partnership with three levels of government. It is a massive infrastructure project and arguably the most significant urban-scale intervention in contemporary Montreal.

The area was originally Faubourg Saint-Laurent, a residential suburb to the walled city in the early 19th century and industrialised by the end of the century. Publishing and printing dominated – the strip between St. Alexandre and Bleury from René-Lévesque south to St. Antoine was known as *Paper Hill*. Square Victoria, elegant in the 19th century, had deteriorated by the 1950s and the 1964 construction of the Tour de la Bourse changed its scale forever.

Excavation for the subway system, completed in 1966, and construction of the Ville-Marie expressway in 1974 ripped apart the Faubourg Saint-Laurent. The 1983 construction of the Palais des congrès on top of the depressed expressway only served to further isolate the no-man's-land it had created. A 1988 charrette and the 1990 *Cité internationale* competition sought ideas as to how to redevelop the area between University and Bleury, from Viger to St. Antoine. Construction of the Centre de commerce mondial de Montréal, completed in 1991, was the first step to revitalization.

The real spur to action was the 1997 government decision to enlarge the Palais des congrès. Property owners, led by the Caisse de dépôt et placement du Québec and in partnership with all levels of government, seized the opportunity to build over the open trench of the expressway at the same time. In so doing they created new public space and reconnected the *quartier* to the downtown core and to Old Montreal, an intriguing example of what the builders describe as "participation of the private sector in a project dedicated solely to the improvement of the public domain."

QIM (QUARTIER INTERNATIONAL DE MONTRÉAL)

Place Riopelle is the heart of the Quartier international de Montréal, a new public square created by building over the open expressway trench and recovering vast areas of parking. A subtle curved line in the hard landscaping of the square is the only clue to the presence of the highway and metro tunnels below. The Centre CDP Capital and the Palais des congrès consciously define the boundaries of this urban room. Trees have been generously planted; Jean-Paul Riopelle's 1969 *La Joute* has been installed surrounded by a fountain.

The other significant intervention in public space is Square Victoria – its original boundaries were restored by rerouting a major city street. Its elegant linear design echoes the formality of the first square built in 1860 – a long sliver of fountain runs down to the urban forest planted in the southern section.

QIM's network of generously-sized, granite-curbed sidewalks and designer Michel Dallaire's street furniture establish a language for the *quartier* that sets it apart from its neighbours – Old Montreal to the south and the downtown core to the north. A line of limestone-clad columns on University creates a new portal to the city. Less apparent but equally important is what you don't see: underground parking, the *RESO* corridors linking buildings to each other and to the metro. QIM is characterized by an attention to detail and a quality of execution that are rare indeed.

Architects	**Daoust Lestage Inc. / Provencher Roy et Associés**
Concept	**Daoust Lestage Inc.**
Client	**Société Quartier international de Montréal**
Completed	**2004**
Address	**from Av. Viger to Rue Saint-Antoine, between Bleury and University**
Métro	**Square-Victoria or Place-d'Armes**
Access	**public**

CENTRE DE COMMERCE MONDIAL DE MONTRÉAL

When one stands on the sidewalk on St. Jacques looking at the façade of the Centre de commerce mondial de Montréal, the scale of this substantial intervention is not immediately apparent – and that is one of the great successes of this 116,000-square-metre project completed in 1991. The developer's concept was to create a horizontal skyscraper by integrating different buildings: the façades of four 19th-century buildings on St. Jacques and one on St. Antoine were retained, while a new structure was built behind. The original lane between the buildings, the Ruelle des Fortifications, was glazed over to make an interior street.

In 2004, when the Quartier international de Montréal was completed, the original intent of the Centre de commerce mondial, to mediate between old and new, and to generate an international precinct, was finally realized. As part of the Quartier international de Montréal, the Passage St. Pierre was added in 2004. Designed by architects Provencher Roy et Associés, it gives access to *RESO*, the underground pedestrian network.

Architects	**Arcop Associates / Provencher Roy et Associés**
Client	**Sociéte de promotion du Centre de commerce mondial de Montréal**
Completed	**1991**
Address	**747 Rue Square-Victoria**
Métro	**Square-Victoria or Place-d'Armes**
Access	**atrium open to the public**

PALAIS DES CONGRÈS

In 1999, after a competition fraught with difficulties, the commission to double the existing 92,000-square-metre area of Montreal's convention centre was awarded to the architectural consortium led by Mario Saia. The technically very complex project, which covers an expressway, connects to a metro station and integrates a block of existing buildings, retained the original 1983 Victor Prus building. The architects' response to a demanding programme was to have each façade reflect the character of its individual street, the most controversial of which has been the coloured-glass west wall facing Place Riopelle. The St. Antoine façade, where the new construction subsumed a series of 19th-century buildings, is unfortunate, as it strips the existing structures of their character.

The interior of the Palais des congrès includes a three-hundred-metre-long tapered "street" running west to east from Place Riopelle to St. Urbain. The north-south corridors that link this main street to St. Antoine are important, as they connect the convention centre to the urban fabric, including Old Montreal to the south. The vast public space of the Hall is fringed by Claude Cormier's *Lipstick Forest* and illuminated by fantastic lozenges of light that stream through the multi-coloured façade.

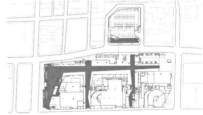

St. Antoine

Architects	**Saia Barbarese Topouzanov / Tétrault Parent Languedoc**
	Aedifica
Independent architectural consultant	**Hal Ingberg**
Landscape architect	**Claude Cormier**
Client	**Société du Palais des Congrès**
Completed	**2003**
Address	**1001, Place Jean-Paul Riopelle**
Métro	**Place-d'Armes**
Access	**public**

CENTRE CDP CAPITAL

Built on massive 30 by 5.4 metre bridge-like steel beams, the headquarters for the Caisse de dépôt et placement du Québec spans the Ville-Marie expressway below it. An integral part of the Quartier international de Montréal, the building is a deliberate gesture to the city on the part of the agency responsible for investing Quebec's pension funds.

The 70,000-square-metre structure, described by its architects as a horizontal skyscraper, links Place Riopelle to the east and Square Victoria to the west via *Le Parquet*, a nine-storey glazed atrium that bridges St. Alexandre. Projecting into the atrium at the sixth and seventh floor is the 560-square-metre trading pod. The new construction wraps itself around three existing buildings, including the 1941 MECO building, whose rooftop garden serves the daycare centre it houses. Here what is most notable is the relationship of each of the buildings' facades to the street and of the building as a whole to the *quartier*.

The building's innovative double-skin technology permits circulation and recycling of air in the ten-centimetre-wide void between the double-glazed curtain wall on the exterior and the single-glazed shutter layer on the interior. The building's "greenness" is discreetly expressed and directed towards providing natural light and fresh air to office workers.

Architects **Gauthier Daoust Lestage Inc. / FABG / Lemay et Associés**
Client **Caisse de dépôt et placement du Québec**
Completed **2003**
Address **1000 Place Jean-Paul Riopelle**
Métro **Square-Victoria or Place-d'Armes**
Access **lobby only – open weekdays during business hours**

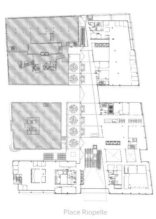

Place Riopelle

UNITY 2

Unity 2 has introduced itself to the Quartier international de Montréal with ease and inventiveness. Built to adjoin the Unity Building (designed by architect David Spence in 1912 and converted to condos in 2001), the L-shaped structure creates an intriguing semi-public interior courtyard. In total, there are five different types of units in Unity 2 – the majority are two-level "flo-thru" units, with windows onto both the courtyard and the street. The complex topological challenge of the building is only hinted at by the very unassuming brick-panel façade.

The wooden-decked courtyard, designed by NIP paysage, is a revelation as one looks through the gate from the street. A dramatic industrial strength exit stair dominates the space on the east side of the courtyard, and five ground-level townhouses front onto it.

Architects	**Atelier Big City**
Landscape architects	**NIP paysage**
Client	**Les Développements D'Arcy McGee Ltée.**
Completed	**2005**
Address	**445 Av. Viger Ouest**
Métro	**Square-Victoria**
Access	**exterior only**

William

Métro Square-Victoria

Darling Foundry

Ottawa

Autoroute Bonaventure

Cité Multimédia, Phase 4

Wellington

Parc des Frères-Charon

Nouve Europa

Prince

Duke

M9

Queen

King

des Soeurs-Grises

Quai de la Commune phase 4

McGill

Cité Multimédia, Phase 8

de la Commune

Brennan

Zone

Nazareth

de la Commune

Mill

0   100 metres

1 minute to walk

FAUBOURG DES RÉCOLLETS

Faubourg des Récollets, immediately to the west of the formerly fortified city, sits at the mouth of the Lachine Canal and was the first area industrialised following the canal's construction in 1825. Originally it included Griffintown, home to the many Irish immigrants who built the canal and who, in the 1880s, worked in the foundries when Montreal was truly the metropolis of Canada.

The Bonaventure expressway, built in 1967, sliced through the *quartier* and with the closure of the Lachine Canal in 1970, the area was largely abandoned by the 1980s. Artists took over the empty factories and warehouses and ultimately were responsible for the regeneration of the *quartier*. *Panique au Faubourg,* a 1997 series of urban installations that included projecting images on the full height of the silos, and the multimedia company Discreet Logic's decision the same year to convert the Weir building into offices marked the turning point for the area.

Cité Multimédia, the section from Ottawa south to the canal, was created by the City of Montreal following its purchase of many of the disused industrial buildings in the early 1990s. Cardinal Hardy / Provencher Roy's master plan for Cité Multimédia prescribed eight phases for the private-public development which houses information technology and multimedia companies.

DARLING FOUNDRY

From 1889 to 1971 the Darling Foundry complex produced industrial equipment. Sold to pump manufacturers, it was finally abandoned in 1991 and sat empty for a decade. The choice of architects Atelier in situ to convert the 1200-square-metre space into a contemporary art centre was a logical one, given their experience with the Zone project in 1997. The architects' strategy was to let the morphology of the building define its reuse – the three-storey-high shop now serves as the centre's multi-functional space, lit by the immense windows that served the factory. Offices are on the second floor; a drywalled area beneath serves as a more traditional gallery. A café/artbar runs the length of the Prince St. façade.

Intervention in this project is simultaneously strong and minimalist, dictated in part by budget constraints but also by a desire to let the building speak for itself. Inset drywall panels define the edges and let the structure show.

In 2006, the adjacent building to the east was converted by the architectural firm L'OEUF to living quarters and studios for Quartier Éphémère's artists-in-residence program.

Architects	**Atelier in situ**
Client	**Quartier Éphémère**
Completed	**2002**
Address	**745 Rue Ottawa**
Métro	**Square-Victoria (+ bus 61 sud to Wellington)**
Access	**open to public during gallery hours /**
	www.quartierephemere.org

FAUBOURG DES RÉCOLLETS

CITÉ MULTIMÉDIA PHASE 4

Cité Multimédia, the government-financed redevelopment of the southern part of Faubourg des Récollets, includes both new construction and projects that integrate existing industrial structures. The architects (who also conceived the master plan for the Cité Multimédia) were adamant about letting the morphology of the industrial neighbourhood determine the form and volume of new construction.

In Phase 4, two Darling Foundry buildings across the street from the foundry proper anchor the north end of the office complex. New construction is very effectively woven into the fabric of early 20th-century brick structures. A garden/courtyard on the Prince side defines an east-west axis through the building's capacious lobby space. Judicious use of materials and careful attention to detail are evident at this ground-floor-level intersection of public and tenant use.

The Bonaventure expressway, defining the western edge of the *quartier*, sits immediately opposite the building's western face. Strong horizontal banding on this side, coming to a distinctive pointed prow on the southwest corner, may announce its presence to those speeding past on the way into the city, but the façade as a whole is awkward when seen from the sidewalk.

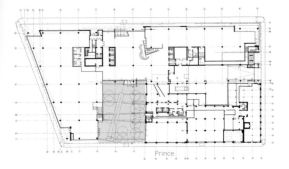

Prince

Architects	**Cardinal Hardy / Provencher Roy et Associés**
Client	**SDM / SITQ Immobilier / SOLIM**
Completed	**2000**
Address	**111 Rue Duke, enter via Prince**
Métro	**Square-Victoria (+ bus 61 sud to Wellington)**
Access	**interior – lobby only**

FAUBOURG DES RÉCOLLETS

A slice of lime in Faubourg des Récollets, this forty-seven-unit condominium project is the first of four phases that will be built at the corner of Wellington and Prince. Acid-green metal frames define individual units on the street side. A large square opening, evoking the *porte-cochère* of a much earlier Montreal housing type, has been cut through the slender building; heavy solid metal doors open to allow entry to the parking below grade. On the interior courtyard side, a bright orange system of metal clapboarding is punctuated by alternating balconies with glazed panels.

In the lobby, which cuts across the building on the short axis, the use of ultra-slick surfaces, back-lit photo-mural panels and a window-wall on the southern edge enlarge a small space.

Architects	**NOMADE**
Client	**Les développements McGill**
Completion	**2007**
Address	**80 Rue Prince**
Métro	**Square-Victoria (+ bus 61 sud to Wellington)**
Access	**exterior only**

FAUBOURG DES RÉCOLLETS

CITÉ MULTIMÉDIA PHASE 8

Like Phase 4 of Cité Multimédia, this building has to present two faces to the world. It must announce the presence of the revitalized *quartier* to those driving along the Bonaventure expressway and it must relate to the late 19th-century scale of the original industrial area. The architects' response was to create two distinct, staggered volumes, linked by a glazed atrium space.

The eight-storey-high west façade on Duke provides all the desired drama with its ceramic-fritted glass screen – remarkable when it reflects winter sunlight or when lit up at night. The smaller volume on Prince is clad in slate-coloured brick on the lower four stories and zinc on the fifth. The lobby joining the two is oriented north-south and is intended to act as the gateway to the neighbourhood. The entrance from Brennan is suitably welcoming but the Prince entry is not as successful.

Architects	**Menkès Shooner Dagenais / Dupuis LeTourneux**
Client	**La Société en commandite Brennan-Duke, Cité Multimédia – Lot 2**
Completed	**2001**
Address	**801 Rue Brennan**
Métro	**Square-Victoria (+ bus 61 sud to Wellington)**
Access	**interior – lobby only**

FAUBOURG DES RÉCOLLETS

ZONE

According to the architects, this project was all about letting the building reveal itself. They deftly recycled a heavy industrial building to serve as the headquarters of a multimedia company. The relentlessly functional exterior was left intact, except for the huge Cor-Ten panels that replace the original doors, with an entry inserted between the two. New steel windows were fitted into the original openings.

The massive interior volumes that once accommodated the manufacture of ship sections – two large halls that were built around an earlier brick factory structure – now house work stations. Material interventions include steel railings, polished concrete floors, and maple doors to define public versus private spaces.

It is not an exaggeration to say that this project generated the revitalization of the Faubourg des Récollets. The energy invested by owner and architects (who worked on site throughout the project) attracted both public and private development to the former industrial area.

Duke

Architects	**Atelier in situ**
Client	**Discreet Logic**
Completed	**1997**
Address	**10 Rue Duke**
Métro	**Square-Victoria (+ bus 61 sud to Wellington)**
Access	**interior – lobby only**

QUAI DE LA COMMUNE PHASE 4

This complex features new construction and reuse of existing buildings, including two early 20th-century warehouses. In all, 325 units of lofts and apartments were built in five phases over six years, in the block between King and des Soeurs-Grises. Of special interest – because of the way it sets itself apart from the typical Montreal housing type – is a series of ten brick and concrete-block rowhouse/studios fronting on King.

Doorways are recessed and fenestration is appropriately industrial. Each building is three storeys tall, with exceptionally high ceilings and large windows overlooking a common interior courtyard.

Architects	**Cardinal Hardy**
Client	**Le Groupe Prével**
Completed	**2003**
Address	**41-59 Rue King**
Métro	**Square-Victoria (+ bus 61 sud to Wellington)**
Access	**exterior only**

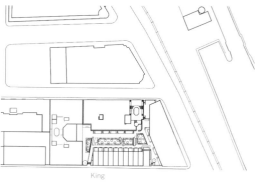

King

NOUVEL EUROPA

The site of the Nouvel Europa, near the foot of McGill St., was a shipyard in the 1800s, then the railhead for the 1923 Union Station – a tiny brick structure that has been integrated into the project. The shape of the new construction is deceptively simple: a large rectangular box with a base and cornice like those of the 19th-century financial and transportation buildings to the north.

The construction is actually two buildings around a central courtyard, the base of which forms the roof slab over the commercial space. Each through-unit apartment has both a street face and a private, courtyard side. Two glazed pedestrian walkways traverse the space; the one at the north end is partially obscured by a semi-transparent screen fritted with black ceramic traces of the rail lines as they were in 1918. This façade is best viewed from further up McGill St.

The Parc des Frères-Charon, north of the site, has been entirely redone by the Ville de Montréal (principal designer Robert Desjardins with architects Affleck + de la Riva). The infrastructure, sidewalks and civic spaces of McGill St. were redesigned by the consortium responsible for the Quartier international de Montréal, providing a long-needed new face for one of Old Montreal's most significant streets.

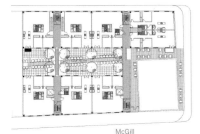

McGill

Architects	**Boutros + Pratte**
Client	**Jean-Pierre Houle**
Completed	**2004**
Address	**50 Rue McGill**
	41 Rue des Soeurs-Grises
	626 Rue d'Youville
Métro	**Square-Victoria (+ bus 61 sud to Wellington)**
Access	**exterior only**

FAUBOURG DES RÉCOLLETS

OLD MONTREAL

There are a few traces of the 18th-century fortified city built by the French but most of the remarkable, densely-built ensemble of greystone buildings that is present-day Old Montreal dates from the 19th century, the era when Montreal was the metropolis of Canada.

Old Montreal was at its lowest ebb in the 1960s. The 1959 opening of the Seaway had diminished the city's role as Canada's principal port and the *quartier* was reduced to rooming houses and warehouses. The 1964 declaration of the sector as an *arrondissement historique* staved off demolition but revitalization was limited to individual restoration projects, mostly to mark Canada's centennial year in 1967, the year of the World's Fair, Expo 67.

Contemporary intervention in Old Montreal is most evident in the recycling and restoration of many 19th-century buildings. From the conversion of convents to apartments in the 1970s to the creation of boutique hotels in the 2000s, rethinking interiors has moved from sensible to chic.

Habitat 67 was built as part of Expo 67 and was the first contemporary intervention in the port. Relocation of the working port to the east in the 1970s meant that much of the infrastructure was abandoned or demolished; the Old Port was created as a separate entity in 1981 by the federal government to oversee redevelopment of the waterfront. The first phase of the revitalization project completed in 1992 created new public urban spaces for cultural and recreational purposes.

East of Berri, Faubourg Québec was a suburb outside the walls in the 18th century and home to the bourgeoisie in the first half of the 19th. The construction of two train stations in the 1880s and 1890s led to complete industrialization of the area which is currently being redeveloped as a residential neighbourhood.

PLACE D'YOUVILLE

To create a new landscape for one of the most historically intense public places in Montreal, Claude Cormier and Cardinal Hardy simply laid what they describe as a "quilt of sidewalks" on top of Place D'Youville. Here, at the site of the founding of Montreal, the archaeological strata are many and run deep at the place where the Petite Rivière ran into the St. Lawrence River. In 1832, the little river was vaulted over and markets were built on top.

Practically – to avoid disturbing artefacts – and philosophically – to not just slavishly recreate history, the design is more about movement across and along the long ribbon that extends from the Centre d'histoire to de la Commune. A granite-paved walk, a "collector of pedestrians," runs down the centre of the Place, evoking the stone conduit of the water collector below. Wooden, limestone and concrete sidewalks cut diagonally across this spine, evoking the domestic, commercial and institutional buildings that line the Place.

The project is only partly complete – the western half of the Place from the Centre d'histoire (a 1902 fire station) to McGill still remains a parking lot.

Landscape architects	**Claude Cormier**
Architects	**Cardinal Hardy**
Client	**Ville de Montréal, Ministère de la Culture et des Communications du Québec**
Completed	**1999**
Address	**Place D'Youville between Place Royale and McGill**
Métro	**Place-d'Armes**
Access	**public**

POINTE-À-CALLIÈRE, MONTREAL MUSEUM OF ARCHAEOLOGY AND HISTORY

The site of the Pointe-à-Callière museum is the triangle of land where de Maisonneuve founded Montreal in 1642 – historic significance so important as to be daunting. The triangular Éperon was built directly on top of more than four centuries of archaeological remains, preserved and exposed below ground. Together, the Éperon building, the crypt under Place Royale and the 1836 Ancienne-Douanes constitute the museum of archaeology and history built in 1992 to celebrate Montreal's 350th anniversary

Clad in the limestone out of which Montreal was built and pierced with vertical slots, the Éperon building succeeds at every level: it respects utterly the streetscape of Old Montreal, pays homage to the port, and alludes to the 1862 Royal Insurance Building which formerly occupied the site. Resolutely contemporary, the structure occupies its corner with absolute assurance, its sliced-cylinder tower a signal to the whole of the Old Port.

The interior contains a theatre dedicated to an audio-visual presentation of Montreal's history, exhibition spaces, offices, and a restaurant on the top floor whose belvedere offers a great view of the Old Port. Access to the crypt and to the former customs house is via a tunnel under Place D'Youville. To provide headroom for the crypt, Place Royale had to be raised above grade, resulting in a curious podium with glazed horizontal slits.

Architects	**Dan S. Hanganu / Provencher Roy (Éperon and crypt)**
	LeMoyne Lapointe Magne (Ancienne-Douanes)
Client	**Ville de Montréal**
Completed	**1992**
Address	**350 Place Royale**
Métro	**Square-Victoria or Place-d'Armes**
Access	**Tuesday to Sunday, Mondays in summer /**
	www.pacmuseum.qc.ca

YOUVILLE PUMPING STATION

The modest 1913 structure that housed Montreal's first electrically-run, waste-water pumping station closed in 1990. Acquired by the Société du Musée d'archéologie, the building was converted and added onto in 1999 to create an interpretation centre for the adjacent Pointe-à-Callière museum. Intervention in the pumping station proper was light-handed, limited to cleaning the brick and painting the three large pumps housed there red.

Construction on a vacant lot to the west of the pumping station provided room for archives, elevator and services, and added office space on the second floor. Matte zinc-titanium panels on the façade frame the yellow-orange Scottish brick of the pumping station; a thoughtful addition to the streetscape in a very visible part of Old Montreal.

Architects	**Dupuis LeTourneux / Beauchamp Bourbeau**
Client	**Pointe-à-Callière, Montreal Museum of Archaeology and History**
Completed	**1999**
Address	**173 Place D'Youville**
Métro	**Place-d'Armes**
Access	**Tuesday to Sunday, Mondays in summer / www.pacmuseum.qc.ca**

OLD PORT

In the 1970s, port operations moved to the east away from Montreal's harbour which had been in use since the 17th century. The many proposals that were put forward on how to redevelop the 53 hectares of the old port succeeded only in creating controversy. Public consultations held in 1985-86 – perhaps the most successful in the city's history – generated the themes upon which the 1990 master plan was based: a port, an historic place and public use.

Letting the history of the place speak for itself meant retaining industrial structures such as Silo #5 and, more pragmatically, keeping the existing rail link to the container port. Traces such as the vestiges of Silo #2's foundations are matter-of-factly integrated. Contemporary interventions like the Pavillon Jacques-Cartier and the ensemble of street furniture, railings, bollards and lamp standards are sober and beautifully scaled.

The first phase of the Old Port revitalization was completed in time for the city's 350th anniversary in 1992. It included excavation and restoration of both the Bonsecours Basin and the western sector at the mouth of the Lachine Canal, as well as construction along the length of de la Commune. The other quays have been refurbished since, including the King Edward pier for the Montreal Science Centre.

The linear park acts simultaneously as access to and relief from Old Montreal for tourists, and as a place to walk and cycle for Montrealers – their window on the river.

Architects	**Cardinal Hardy et Associés / Peter Rose / Jodoin Lamarre Pratte et Associés (master plan)**
Completed	**1993**
Client	**Société du Vieux-Port de Montréal**
Address	**mouth of Lachine Canal to Faubourg Québec**
Métro	**Square-Victoria or Place-d'Armes or Champ-de-Mars**
Access	**public**

OLD PORT

Maison des Éclusiers

An integral part of the 1992 Old Port project, the Maison des Éclusiers offers a spectacular view of the mouth of the Lachine Canal and its locks. The industrial language of the pavilion is clearly drawn from the infrastructure of the port – part of the overall intent to let the contemporary construction speak to the port's early 20th-century history. The pavilion houses a café-terrasse in the summer.

Architects	**Cardinal Hardy et Associés**
Client	**Société du Vieux-Port de Montréal**
Completed	**1993**
Address	**Rue McGill at de la Commune**
Métro	**Square-Victoria or Place-d'Armes or Champ-de-Mars**
Access	**seasonal – open end of May to end of September**

Montreal Science Centre

Two immense sheds – with a total area of 500,000 square metres – on the King Edward pier were transformed into a science interpretation centre and parking facility. The volumes were kept simple, and the new exterior double skin is rhythmic and industrial in scale. The service road between the two, an extension of St. Laurent, is lined with recycled containers that open up as shops in the summer.

Architects **Gauthier Daoust Lestage Inc. / FABG**
Client **Société du Vieux-Port de Montréal**
Completed **2000**
Address **Quai King Edward**
Métro **Place-d'Armes**
Access **open every day /**
www.centredessciencesdemontreal.com

OLD PORT

Pavillon Jacques-Cartier

Constructed on the foundations of the great long shed that once stood on this pier, the pavilion evokes the maritime language of the port. An enfilade of steel masts runs the length of the quay, its tension cables supporting a raised walkway. The enclosed large open space for seasonal events is almost entirely glazed, its structure exposed. To the visitor walking down Place Jacques-Cartier from Notre-Dame, the pavilion is the clearest possible signal of the contemporary nature of the Old Port.

Architects	**Cardinal Hardy / Cayouette-Chartrand**
Client	**Société du Vieux-Port de Montréal**
Completed	**1992**
Address	**Quai Jacques-Cartier**
Métro	**Champ-de-Mars**
Access	**seasonal – open end of May to end of September**

Pavillon du bassin Bonsecours

The Bonsecours Basin was excavated in 1992 and a skating rink was built. The skating pavilion is deceptively simple and with its playful allusion to the 19th-century domes of the old city, a contrast to the industrial language of other Old Port projects. Deliberately over-scaled, its domed roof holds its own in the landscape and signals that the Bonsecours Basin is more park than port.

Architects **Luc Laporte**
Client **Société du Vieux-Port de Montréal**
Completed **1992**
Address **Rue de la Commune Est (Parc du bassin Bonsecours)**
Métro **Champ-de-Mars**
Access **public**

SQUARE DALHOUSIE

Faubourg Québec was a "suburb" outside the original walled city of Montreal, built at the gate to the road to Quebec City. The whole area – including the original Dalhousie Square – was destroyed by fire in 1852. In the late 19th century, the nascent railways built stations and railyards – the first train to leave for the west departed from Dalhousie Station in 1886.

Square Dalhousie is a new public space that sits on these invisible layers of history and acts as entryway to the new Faubourg Québec, a 70-hectare redevelopment project by the Société de développement de Montréal. Defined to the north by the former Dalhousie Station and to the south by new residential construction, the square is a narrative: it traces the location of the original fortification walls and incorporates vestiges of the railway era. A sculpture by Jocelyne Alloucherie commemorates the Quebec gate.

Dalhousie Station was imaginatively recycled to house a circus school in 1986 by architect Vinney Bélanger.

The Notre-Dame viaduct – accessible via a stairway to the east of the station – was rebuilt by architects Dupuis LeTourneux with Saia Barbarese in 1997. Described as a "bridge building," it is intended as both roadway and outlook, with a view of the whole *faubourg* and the river beyond.

Architects **Ville de Montréal (principal designer Robert Desjardins)**
Client **Ville de Montréal**
Completed **2004**
Address **Rue Berri south of Rue Notre-Dame**
Métro **Champ-de-Mars**
Access **public**

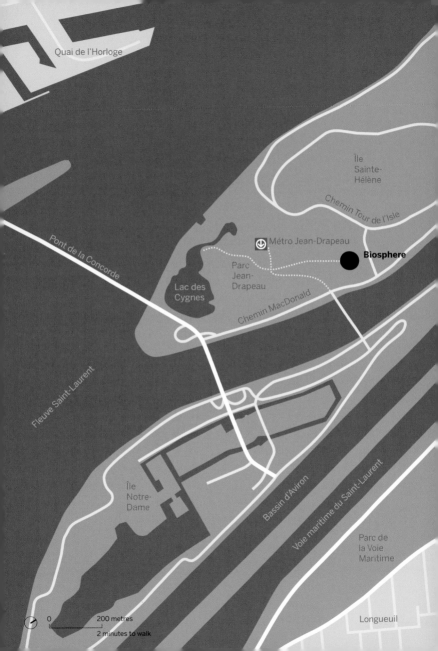

PARC JEAN-DRAPEAU

BIOSPHERE

Île Ste. Hélène has been used as a park by Montrealers since 1874, accessible first by ferry then via the Jacques Cartier bridge built in 1930. Frederick Todd, the landscape architect responsible for the area around Beaver Lake on Mount Royal, redesigned the island in the 1930s when, as part of the city's make-work projects at the height of the Depression, a swimmers' pavilion and a tower were built next to the 1820 citadel constructed by the British.

Île Ste. Hélène and the man-made Île Notre-Dame were the site of Expo 67, the World's Fair that marked Canada's centennial. Very little remains of that glorious summer and, with the exception of the Biosphere, that which does remain is no longer recognizable.

The islands (renamed Parc Jean-Drapeau to honour the mayor who brought Expo 67 to Montreal) now include many recreational activities. Île Ste. Hélène has a swimming pool complex and La Ronde, an amusement park that first opened as part of Expo 67; Île Notre-Dame is home to the Grand Prix racetrack and the Olympic rowing basin.

BIOSPHERE

Intervention or conservation? A spectacular fire in 1976 destroyed the acrylic skin of Buckminster Fuller's geodesic dome, built as the American pavilion for Expo 67. It sat empty and rusting until 1992. Environment Canada undertook to reopen the structure as an interpretation centre focused on the idea of water, and specifically on the St. Lawrence River ecosystem. The architectural competition required that the existing platform structure be maintained.

Éric Gauthier's design is utterly respectful – both of the mandate and of Fuller – and at the same time assertive in its own right. The paradox of having to provide inwardly-focused exhibition space while maximizing natural light and the dome's presence is neatly resolved. What Gauthier gives us is the *experience* of moving through the structure. From a low pavilion at grade, one moves up around a central courtyard to the belvedere, all the while being engulfed by the iconic skeleton of Fuller's dome.

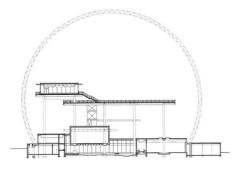

Architects	**Blouin Faucher Aubertin Brodeur Gauthier / Desnoyers Mercure et Associés**
Client	**Environment Canada and Ville de Montréal**
Completed	**1994**
Address	**160 Chemin Tour de l'Isle**
Métro	**Jean-Drapeau**
Access	**Tuesday to Sunday, Mondays in summer / www.biosphere.ec.gc.ca**

PARC JEAN-DRAPEAU

Pavillon du Jardin des Premières-Nations

Insectarium

Jardin botanique

Sherbrooke

Parc Maisonneuve

Bourbonnière

d'Orléans

Charlemagne

Jeanne-d'Arc

Pierre de Coubertin

Métro Pie-IX

Métro Viau

Hochelaga

Pie-IX

Desjardins

de la Salle

Letourneux

Bennet

Aird

Sicard

Leclaire

Théodore

Saint-Clément

Viau

de Rouen

Johnson & Johnson

Maison de la culture Maisonneuve

Ontario

La Fontaine

Morgan

William-David

0   200 metres
2 minutes to walk

HOCHELAGA-MAISONNEUVE /
JARDIN BOTANIQUE

Once a tiny village, Hochelaga was industrialized very rapidly in the last quarter of the 19th century and annexed by the city of Montreal in 1883. The 1905 construction by Canadian Pacific Railways of the immense Angus Shops in neighbouring Rosemont made the northern section of Hochelaga an enclave of workers' housing.

A group of wealthy industrialist-landowners resisted the annexation of the eastern section of Hochelaga and created the town of Maisonneuve. By 1915, huge factories like American Can and Dominion Textile had made the area "Canada's Pittsburgh." A remarkable, ambitious (and ultimately ruinously expensive) 1910 plan was intended to make Maisonneuve a model city, strongly influenced by the American "City Beautiful" movement. Evidence of this plan can still be seen in the width of Morgan Blvd. and the significant public buildings that include a city hall, public baths, and a market. The First World War brought financial collapse to Maisonneuve, and the town was annexed to Montreal in 1918.

The Botanical Gardens (Jardin Botanique) were established in Parc Maisonneuve in the 1930s – the work of landscape architect Henry Teuscher and horticulturalist Frère Marie-Victorin. The park is also the site of the 1976 Olympics installations, including the infamous stadium, the "Big O."

JOHNSON & JOHNSON

This "Post-Modern" building is undoubtedly less daring today than when it was completed in 1986. The true significance of this project, however, lies in the fact that the architects convinced Johnson & Johnson to remain in the working-class/industrial neighbourhood where the company had erected its first Canadian factory in 1919, in an era when corporations were eager to build glass and granite towers downtown.

Two brick buildings – one dating from 1912 and the other from 1926 – were converted from industrial to office use, and a new central block was constructed, creating a courtyard. The arcade at the entry is a clear allusion to both the residential *porte-cochère* typical of Montreal row housing and the Beaux-Arts buildings that characterize the Maisonneuve district. Inside the central courtyard, references to industrial architecture abound: the trusses on the *passerelles*; the concrete-block exit-stair silo; the use of brick and factory-like fenestration. A three-storey-high glazed lobby, the grand hall, spreads across the width of the new pavilion.

In an interesting juxtaposition, the housing project directly opposite, Les habitations de Rouen, was designed by Cayouette Saia / Saia Barbarese in 1993.

 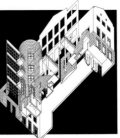

Architects	**Cayouette, Saia et Associés**
Client	**Johnson & Johnson Inc. (now owned by Vidéotron Télécom)**
Completed	**1986**
Address	**2155 Boul. Pie-IX**
Métro	**Pie-IX (+ bus 139 sud)**
Access	**exterior only**

MAISON DE LA CULTURE MAISONNEUVE

If the Johnson & Johnson conversion on nearby Pie-IX was remarkable for the gesture it made to the neighbourhood in 1986, this intervention in former Fire Station No. 45 demonstrates how much the *quartier* has changed in twenty years. The shift is further illustrated by the very lively debate that occurred about the Maison de la culture taking over the fire station space from another artistic organization.

While conversion of fire stations has become commonplace in Montreal, this is a particularly elegant example. The new construction to the south of the original 1895 building proclaims itself as confidently different. The glazed structure on a grey brick base houses a dance space, while the original fire station garage accommodates a multi-functional performance and exhibition space.

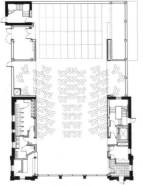

Ontario Est

Architects	**FABG**
Client	**arrondissement Mercier-Hochelaga-Maisonneuve**
Completed	**2005**
Address	**4200 Rue Ontario Est**
Métro	**Pie-IX (+ bus 139 sud)**
Access	**open Thursday to Sunday afternoons**

PAVILLON DU JARDIN DES PREMIÈRES-NATIONS

This pavilion, reached by a path through the woods, was built to commemorate the 300th anniversary of the *Grand Paix*, the treaty signed with First Nations peoples in 1701. Its undulating canopy of thin concrete, clad in lead-covered copper, follows the topography of the pathway, and the long lean curve of the structure appears as a screen between the deciduous and coniferous sections of the forest. The pavilion is built partially below grade, so as to further submerge it into the landscape. Materials that were clearly chosen for their durability, such as concrete formed with wood slats, are juxtaposed with natural woods and vertical glass showcases. The effect is at the same time transparent, inviting and poetic.

Architects **Saucier + Perrotte**
Client **Jardin botanique de Montréal / Ville de Montréal**
Completed **2001**
Address **Jardin botanique de Montréal, 4101 Rue Sherbrooke Est**
Métro **Pie-IX**
Access **open every day, except Mondays in winter (admission fee)**
www2.ville.montreal.qc.ca/jardin

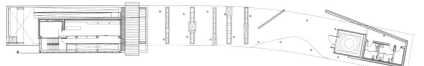

JARDIN BOTANIQUE

STE. MARIE

Ste. Marie is the original name for an industrial neighbourhood known as *Faubourg à m'lasse* from the mid-19th to the mid-20th centuries, where tobacco, textile and food factories were located, as well as housing for the workers. Industry vacated the area in the 1950s. The late 1960s urban renewal scheme put forward by the then mayor Jean Drapeau entailed demolition of more than a thousand housing units with the intent of creating a *Cité des ondes,* a whole *quartier* devoted to the telecommunications industry, running from La Fontaine Park south to the river. Maison Radio-Canada was built and opened in 1973, but the area around it was razed for parking, and the rest of the scheme was never realized.

The Gay Village is a relatively recent name for the western part of Ste. Marie on Ste. Catherine between St. Hubert and Papineau where, starting from a cluster of restaurants and clubs in the 1990s, the presence of the gay community has revitalized the whole neighbourhood.

USINE C

After twenty years of wandering, the avant-garde performance troupe Carbone 14 chose a former jam factory – Usine Raymond – as its permanent home. A tall brick chimney capped with a sculpture by Richard Purdy signals the presence of the cultural complex in the neighbourhood, known in the early 20th century as *Faubourg à m'lasse*.

A new theatre space clad in recycled brick was added to the north of the existing structure, which runs east-west on Lalonde, thus defining the circulation along two intersecting axes. A glazed node at this intersection links new construction to old, both horizontally and vertically. This node overlooks an interior courtyard and a spiral stair that leads to offices and the entry to the auditorium. The 450-seat theatre is a large black box that can be reconfigured for different seating formats. The ramp leading to the west entry on Visitation becomes a *passerelle* which traverses the former boiler room below, now home to a lively café.

Materials are everything here. The contrast between the muscularity of the exposed concrete and the delicacy of glass is executed with a beguiling simplicity.

de la Visitation

Architects	**Saucier + Perrotte**
Client	**Carbone 14**
Completed	**1995**
Address	**1345 Rue Lalonde**
Métro	**Beaudry**
Access	**Monday to Saturday / www.usine-c.com**

THÉÂTRE ESPACE LIBRE

A neat solution to a problem common to many small cultural organizations. The theatre company Espace Libre had outgrown the former fire station that had been its home for twenty years and wanted to renovate to provide rehearsal and performance space for itself and two other theatre companies. A very tight budget and a tighter site meant excising part of the building, filling it with a modern box, and adding floors below grade and on the roof. Of the original fire station, only the front façade and part of the south façade, the party wall, and the hose tower remain.

The main performance space occupies the whole of the ground floor, accessible via the original garage doors. Each theatre company has its own rehearsal and office spaces with separate entry doors; the stairway leading to them is visible through the glazed south façade. The zig-zagged curtain wall that wraps around the east face is operable, providing natural ventilation. The fire hall turned theatre is at its best at night when the light behind the glass façade glows a greeny-yellow.

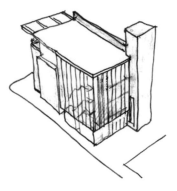

Architects **Lapointe Magne et Associés**
Client **Théâtre Espace Libre**
Completed **2002**
Address **1945 Rue Fullum**
Métro **Frontenac**
Access **exterior only / www.espacelibre.qc.ca**

STE. MARIE

QUARTIER LATIN

For the short twenty-year period between the two world wars, St. Denis St. was the cultural heart of francophone Montreal. Home to the École des Hautes Études Commerciales and the medical and law faculties of the nascent Université de Montréal, the area around St. Denis attracted theatres and cafés. The Bibliothèque Saint-Sulpice, Montreal's first purpose-built French-language library, opened here in 1915.

In 1943, the Université de Montréal moved to the north slopes of Mount Royal and the once-elegant greystones (dating from the 19th century when the bourgeoisie made their homes there) emptied out. The Quartier Latin deteriorated badly – revival started only in the 1960s with quirky stores and restaurants. The creation of the new Université du Québec à Montréal (UQÀM) in 1969 meant the return of people to the neighbourhood but to some rather dire brutalist concrete buildings anchored to the Berri-UQÀM metro station.

The interior-focused UQÀM buildings made public spaces all the more important. However, Place Émilie-Gamelin, designed in 1992, has not been realized as intended despite its significance, sitting as it does on top of the nexus of the metro system. Square Viger, a once-treed Victorian square that was demolished and covered in concrete when the depressed Ville-Marie expressway was extended in 1981, awaits an overhaul.

Cultural institutions emblematic of late 20th-century Quebec such as the Cinémathèque, the Grande Bibliothèque, and the Centre Pierre-Péladeau have infused the *quartier* with energy and renewed purpose.

CENTRE D'ARCHIVES DE MONTRÉAL

Quebec's cultural history is archived in a network of regional centres and in the Grande Bibliothèque. At the Centre d'archives de Montréal, located in a complex of buildings that occupies a city block fronting onto Viger, researchers have access to Montreal documents dating back to the 17th century.

Dan S. Hanganu / Provencher Roy won the competition organized in 1997 to reuse and add on to four existing buildings on the site including the 1911 École des hautes études commerciales building and the 1870 Maison Jodoin.

There is a sense of revelation as the visitor moves from the imposing original entry lobby up the stairs and into the bold six-storey glazed atrium at the core. On the north side of the atrium the original doors now float in a mullionless wall of glass, and beyond, an interior courtyard leads to the consultation room. This space for researchers is housed in the wonderful cast-iron fantasy of the former 1916 Musée industriel et commercial. Here, as everywhere in this project, the attitude of combining new with old is straightforward – as demonstrated by the circular stair that has been inserted with clarity and assurance

Not to be overlooked is the new storage structure, seen best from Labelle, a grey zinc box with an elegant metal trellis for vines.

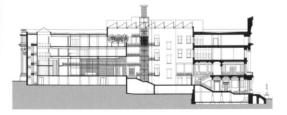

Architects **Dan S. Hanganu / Provencher Roy et Associés**
Client **Société immobilière du Québec**
Completed **1999**
Address **535 Av. Viger Est**
Métro **Champ-de-Mars**
Access **interior lobby only – Tuesday through Sunday / www.banq.qc.ca**

PAVILLON DE DESIGN DE L'UQÀM

In stark contrast to the massive concrete hulks that the university built in the 1970s, this complex has added cachet to the UQÀM urban campus. The Pavillon de design programme included studios, classrooms and offices for the schools of design de l'environnement and graphic design as well as exhibition space for the Centre de design.

The building fronts onto Sanguinet, with a finger stretching down to Ste. Catherine. The main volume extends back from Sanguinet along Boisbriand. Eight storeys high, it is organized around a daylit open core, through which passages cross and stairways mount. This is not a simple building – there are many layers and the best way to see the building is to start at the top at the tiny roof garden and walk down. The ground floor is the public space, with the Centre de design gallery ideally positioned for access from the street. Like most UQÀM buildings, this pavilion is linked by tunnel to the metro.

The design pavilion is robust and intended for hard use. Materials are industrial– steel mesh, steel checkerplate, exposed concrete – and are employed exuberantly, with careful detailing throughout.

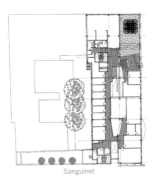

Sanguinet

Architects	**Dan S. Hanganu**
Client	**UQÀM**
Completed	**1996**
Address	**1440 Rue Sanguinet**
Métro	**Berri-UQAM**
Access	**university hours**

CINÉMATHÈQUE QUÉBÉCOISE

Reusing two former school buildings on de Maisonneuve – and more importantly inserting new volumes into the space between the two – gave the Cinémathèque québécoise (an important repository of Québécois films) a presence in the Quartier Latin. The entry, a cube described by the architect as a light-box, sits poised slightly back from the sidewalk, yet at night seems to extend into the street. A glass and metal box projects out from the face of the entry cube and serves as a translucent projection screen: people moving across the ramp immediately behind it are suddenly actors on screen.

To enter the building, the visitor crosses a metal bridge over a narrow gap. Inside, an agora – a balcony of raked seating – cantilevers out at mid-level in the volume of the entry box allowing visitors to view projections on the screen on the north wall. The palette is deliberately black and white, the materials are sleek, in contrast to the exposed concrete frame that delineates the boundary between old and new construction.

To the west of the entry, a courtyard leads to a café folded into the heart of the building. A médiathèque below grade is lit by natural light from the courtyard. Exhibition galleries, a small theatre, and a video projection room are in the new volume; offices are in the former Jeanne Mance school to the east.

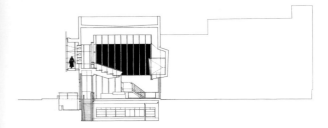

Architects **Saucier + Perrotte**
Client **Cinémathèque québécoise**
Completed **1997**
Address **355 Boul. de Maisonneuve Est**
Métro **Berri-UQAM**
Access **Tuesday to Sunday / www.cinematheque.qc.ca**

QUARTIER LATIN

GRANDE BIBLIOTHÈQUE

Significant both for its architecture and its content, the project for Quebec's new library was subjected to constant scrutiny – from the international architectural competition in 2000 to its inauguration in 2005. Few architects from outside Quebec have been given such major commissions in the last twenty-five years and few projects have been as culturally important.

The library is a great long rectangular metal box (33,000 square metres, six storeys high), clad in pale green ceramic-coated glass louvres; it connects both to the street and to the metro one floor below. At street level, there are two main entrances, at either end of a long public passage flooded with natural light.

On the inside, the building is generous and eminently readable. The ease with which one moves up through the central core and around the perimeter is remarkable given the complexity of the programme.

The library's two principal holdings – the lending/reference collection and the *collection Québécoise* which includes everything ever published in Quebec – are contained in two immense and beautiful wood-slatted volumes, one at the centre of the building and the other at the northern end. These *chambres de bois* (inspired by the novelist Anne Hébert) subtly use wood as a backdrop to reading spaces and study carrels.

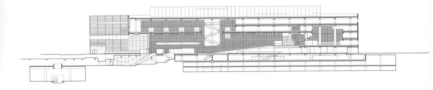

Architects **Patkau / Croft Pelletier / Menkès Shooner Dagenais**
Client **Bibliothèque et Archives nationales du Québec**
Completed **2005**
Address **475 Boul. de Maisonneuve Est**
Métro **Berri-UQAM**
Access **Tuesday through Sunday / www.banq.qc.ca**

Fairmount

Plaza Laurier

Laurier

🔵 Métro Laurier

Édouard-Charles

Saint-Joseph

Jeanne-Mance

de l'Esplanade

Théâtre Espace Go

Villeneuve

Pontiac

Resther

Boyer

du Mont-Royal

🔵 Métro Mont-Royal

Maison Coloniale

Marie-Anne

Pavot rouge

Parc Mont-Royal

Parc Jeanne-Mance

À l'ombre de Paris

Rachel

Box House

du Parc

Duluth

Saint-Laurent

Saint-Dominique

Coloniale

de Bullion

de l'Hôtel-De-Ville

Laval

Henri-Julien

Drolet

Saint-Denis

Rivard

Berri

de Chateaubriand

Saint-Hubert

Saint-Christophe

Saint-André

de Mentana

du Parc La Fontaine

Bagg

Napoléon

Roy

Tower House

des Pins

Square Saint-Louis

Institut de tourisme et d'hôtellerie du Québec

Prince-Arthur

🔵 Métro Sherbrooke

University

Durocher

Hutchison

Jeanne-Mance

Sainte-Famille

Saint-Urbain

Milton

Sherbrooke

Labrecque

Amherst

Complexe des sciences de l'UQÀM

VII-Plex

Saint-Norbert

Clark

Ontario

Sanguinet

Savoie

Saint-Timothée

Président-Kennedy

🔵 Métro Place-des-Arts

Métro Saint-Laurent 🔵

Métro Berri-UQAM 🔵

de Maisonneu

0   200 metres
2 minutes to walk

PLATEAU MONT-ROYAL

The Plateau is a densely-built neighbourhood of rowhouses, an *enfilade* of curved staircases that extends from Sherbrooke north to the railway tracks at Van Horne, east to Frontenac and west to the mountain. Built almost entirely in the boom period from 1890 to 1930 – initially to house those who worked in the quarries at the Plateau's northern edge – the area became Montreal's hottest neighbourhood in the late 20th century. Young Montrealers rent flats (Montreal still has the highest proportion of rental housing in North America) or buy condos in a part of town where they can walk out the door and into a restaurant in less than a minute.

St. Laurent Blvd. was often the first home to immigrants arriving in the port of Montreal and the street's character has always reflected that fact. Geographically, "the Main" divides the city into east and west; traditionally, it was the border between French and English neighbourhoods.

Mont-Royal slices through the *quartier* leading to the mountain and is the dividing line between the four original villages that were amalgamated to make up the Plateau. The street has been revitalized since the 1990s, principally through the efforts of merchants.

There is very little green space or public space in this area of the city. Square St. Louis, an elegant 1879 residential square, and La Fontaine Park, at the southern edge, are welcome exceptions.

MAISON COLONIALE

A house that stands apart from all others. Jacques Rousseau's personal exploration of the city and of architecture – how a house embodies both a city's past and the moment at which it is built – takes form in the house he built for himself on the *tête d'îlôt* of the block formed by Coloniale and de Bullion on Marie-Anne. Its twin, square concrete towers and the courtyard between them are a play on the idea of inside-outside; its four levels move up from public to private. In fact, the house was originally intended as studio, office, exhibition space – and home.

In the interior, the floorplates are not continuously connected to the walls, and partitions are limited to cubicles where needed. In the summer, garage doors at the third level open to the outside at either end of the connecting bridge.

Execution is not perfect. There is an unfinished quality to the construction that has not always served the house well, but much is forgiven, in light of the *beau geste*.

Architects	**Jacques Rousseau**
Client	**private**
Completed	**1990**
Address	**4333 Av. Coloniale**
Métro	**Mont-Royal**
Access	**exterior only**

PLATEAU MONT-ROYAL

HOUSES ON THE PLATEAU

The Montreal triplex – a three-storey rowhouse with exterior staircase – is a strong housing type that has created a robust streetscape in many *quartiers*. The best new domestic architecture in the Plateau integrates without mimicry; it satisfies the City of Montreal's requirements to respect the city's built heritage, while injecting new energy into the neighbourhood.

Constrained by a very narrow site, VII-Plex breaks the triplex typology by building a staircase in the middle of the long axis and a unit on either side. The existing private laneway was landscaped to provide access to the entry; its garden gives all seven apartments a green and leafy view. The generously-sized blue steel balconies extend the space of each apartment.

Tower House is actually two towers with two units each, covering ninety per cent of its corner lot. The insertion of the tiny courtyard allows large corner windows in each unit: the bridge spanning the courtyard at the third-storey level forms part of the fire escape.

VII-Plex
2120 Rue Clark

Tower House
3776-82 Av. Laval

Architects **Atelier Big City**
Completed **1991**
Métro **Saint-Laurent**

Architects **BUILD**
Completed **1997**
Métro **Sherbrooke**

À l'ombre de Paris was built on a vacant lot that stayed that way for a long time because the seven-storey Paris Star building (formerly a textile factory) on the west side of Coloniale, blocked all available light. A duplex – in this case a house and studio – is built entirely around a large square lightwell at the core. The exterior, of dark grey block, is discreet with its small-scale entry and recessed garage door behind a bright yellow gate.

Box House is remarkable because it sits at the intersection of a lane and an alley, so it sits quite literally in the middle of the street. Described by the architects as "a box with metal appendages," the house stacks living space above studio with windows carefully sliced to privilege the view to Mount Royal.

Pavot Rouge is located on the same alley. This small (ninety-eight square metres) insertion is built on top of an existing garage, wrapped in a glorious orange-red ceramic-glazed brick and topped off by a green roof.

À l'ombre de Paris
4227-29 Rue Coloniale

Box House
4056 Rue Saint-Christophe

Pavot rouge
4274 Rue Saint-Christophe

Architects	**YH2**
Completed	**2001**
Métro	**Mont-Royal**

Architects	**BUILD**
Completed	**1999**
Métro	**Mont-Royal**

Architects	**YH2**
Completed	**2007**
Métro	**Mont-Royal**

COMPLEXE DES SCIENCES DE L'UQÀM

Montreal's four universities went on a building spree in the late 1990s – UQÀM (Université du Québec à Montréal) went so far as to construct a whole precinct for its science buildings. In 1997, on a mostly-vacant block, Saia Barbarese was responsible for the first project – the elliptical Pavillon President-Kennedy – along with the restoration of the 1917 École Technique at the corner of Jeanne-Mance and Sherbrooke.

The campus was completed in 2005 by the construction of a series of buildings and a coherent web of paths and public spaces. Saia Barbarese Topouzanov conceived the ensemble of pavilions to house classrooms, laboratories, research areas, student residences and the "Cœur des sciences," a former forge used by École Technique students, now converted to a public meeting space. All the pavilions are built in the yellow brick characteristic of early 20th-century Montreal institutions. The use of coloured glass throughout produces fascinating plays of light – least successful perhaps in the most visible pavilion on Sherbrooke.

The act of walking through the campus from Sherbrooke to President-Kennedy gives one a sense of containment, of being set apart in an enclosed world.

Architects	**Saia Barbarese Topouzanov / Tétreault Parent Languedoc**
Landscape architects	**Claude Cormier**
Client	**Université du Québec à Montréal**
Completed	**2005**
Address	**200 Rue Sherbrooke Ouest (Pavillon Sherbrooke); 141 Av. du Président-Kennedy (Sciences biologiques)**
Métro	**Place-des-Arts**
Access	**public**

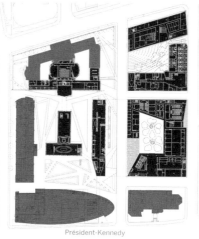

Président-Kennedy

PLATEAU MONT-ROYAL

INSTITUT DE TOURISME ET D'HÔTELLERIE DU QUÉBEC

1974 was the first year that the Société d'architecture de Montréal – in what was to become a Save Montreal annual tradition – awarded Oranges and Lemons to celebrate the best and worst projects built in the preceding year. The very first Lemon went to the original incarnation of the ITHQ, a 1970 Brutalist eleven-storey tower on a concrete podium entirely out of scale with the neighbourhood.

Thirty years later, the much-maligned building housing the province's hotel and tourism school was completely renovated. A new double skin was wrapped around the structure, giving it a new face and at the same time preheating the air brought into the building. The design focus has been on the elevations – each elevation on the tower is different from the others. On de Rigaud and on de Malines there are balconies for the hotel rooms; on the St. Denis façade, the glazing of the tower is saw-toothed green and yellow. Fritted glazing across the full width of the podium on St. Denis announces the ITHQ's presence; this side has been opened up at the sidewalk level and glazed, allowing passersby to see into the restaurant and lobby.

Architects	**Lapointe Magne et Associés / Aedifica**
Client	**Société immobilière du Québec**
Completed	**2005**
Address	**3535 Rue Saint-Denis**
Métro	**Sherbrooke**
Access	**interior – lobby areas only**

THÉÂTRE ESPACE GO

In 1994, the Espace Go theatre company elected to build a new venue on a vacant lot in a relatively quiet stretch of St. Laurent, rather than reuse an existing building as did many other small companies at the time. This crisp and collected building inserted itself gracefully into the streetscape and looks as if it had always been there.

Sections of Indiana-limestone clapboard bracket the full-height glazed opening that reveals the foyer, lobby and bar at ground level and offices above. Looking in from the sidewalk, the arcade of thin structural columns and the poetry-etched glass create a certain distance between pedestrian and theatre-goer. Once inside, the impression is reversed and the sidewalk feels like part of the foyer.

The three-storey-high theatre space is completely flexible and seats about 250 people depending on the configuration for the particular production. A rehearsal space contiguous to the main space opens onto Clark, one street to the west. Atypically, there is no laneway in this block, and access to the truck dock is through a *porte-cochère* on the St. Laurent façade.

Architects **Blouin Faucher Aubertin Brodeur Gauthier**
Client **Théâtre Espace Go**
Completed **1995**
Address **4890 Boul. St-Laurent**
Métro **Laurier**
Access **Tuesday to Saturday / www.espacego.com**

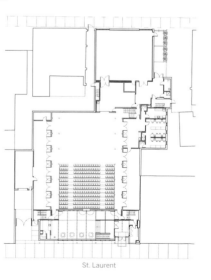

St. Laurent

PLATEAU MONT-ROYAL

PLAZA LAURIER

When Plaza Laurier was constructed in the early 1990s, this mixed industrial and residential area known as Mile End was considered marginal and badly in need of revitalization. This project for affordable housing built in several phases not only restored coherence to three city blocks, it did so in a respectful, solidly modern fashion.

The first phase on Henri-Julien is L-shaped and brick-clad, built on top of a privately-run parking structure, whose revenues help fund the project. Two-storey units at grade have their own entrances and are intended for families; the upper three storeys are for seniors and couples. The entrance to the upper units is a two-storey-high void; it adjoins a pedestrian access path leading to a park and school. A communal garden is located on the plot defined by the building's L-shape.

Henri-Julien

Architects **Boutros + Pratte**
Client **Office municipal d'Habitation de Montréal**
Completed **1994**
Address **5172 Av. Henri-Julien (phase 1)**
Métro **Laurier**
Access **exterior only**

Deville

Parc Jean-Rivard

7e Avenue

8e Avenue

Saint-Michel

Complexe
environnemental
de Saint-Michel

Jean-Rivard

**115 Studios –
Cirque
du Soleil**

d'Hérelle

**Cirque
du Soleil**

Michel-Jourdant

des Regrattiers

TOHU

Paul-Boutet

**École
nationale
de cirque**

Crémazie

Jarry

Autoroute métropolitaine

Henri-Brien

2e Avenue

6e Avenue

8e Avenue

9e Avenue

10e Avenue

Tillemont

Parc
Nicolas-
Tillemont

Villeray

de Lorimier

des Érables

Sagard

Louis-Hémon

des Écores

Louis-Hébert

d'Iberville

Molson

1re Avenue

L.-O.-David

Everett

0   200 metres

2 minutes to walk

Métro D'Iberville

Jean-Talon

ST. MICHEL

St. Michel was a village, still home to farmers until the end of the Second World War, although the dominant industry was the quarries, established as early as the 1750s. By the 1950s, the Miron and Francon quarries were immense, producing gravel and sand. Miron's massive cement factory fed the building boom in downtown Montreal and the 1959 construction of the St. Lawrence Seaway, but its tall chimneys made the neighbourhood a hot-spot of pollution. Closed in 1968, the Miron quarry became a waste-disposal site, which was itself closed in 2000 and converted to the St. Michel environmental complex.

Cirque du Soleil's 1995 decision to build its headquarters on the edge of the Miron quarry – and the subsequent construction of an amazing collection of buildings dedicated to the circus arts – has helped to revitalize St. Michel. However, the potential for the Cité des arts du cirque to be a truly cohesive campus remains unrealized.

CIRQUE DU SOLEIL

Cirque du Soleil is the Quebec troupe that grew from a big-top in Montreal's Old Port in the 1980s to shows that tour the world and permanent installations in Las Vegas and Orlando. This international headquarters houses rehearsal space as well as costume and prop studios for all Cirque productions.

The choice of site – it's built on the southern edge of the now-closed Miron quarry/dump – was seen as adventurous in the mid-1990s. Conceived from the outset as an integral part of the adjacent St. Michel Environmental Complex and park, Hanganu's building was a strong statement in a marginal landscape.

Built as a "work in progress" (its first extension was undertaken during the original construction), the structure has since been enlarged twice by FABG architects. Clad in corrugated metal siding, it is now industrial in scale as well as materials. The most interesting façade is still the fragmented north side that overlooks the Place du Chapiteau and the Miron quarry beyond; that façade and the whimsical steel-mesh-draped main entry are the strongest exterior evidence of Hanganu's playfulness. (Walk around the building to experience the scale, volume and complexity.)

Inside the building (visitors can enter only as far as the lobby), a massive skylit corridor is an interior street over which catwalks and balconies project. Here, performers, artisans and management are brought into constant contact with one another.

Architects	**Dan S. Hanganu (original building) / FABG (additions)**
Client	**Cirque du Soleil**
Completed	**1997 (original building), 2000 and 2007 (additions)**
Address	**8400 2ᵉ Avenue**
Métro	**d'Iberville (+ bus 94 nord)**
Access	**exterior and lobby only**

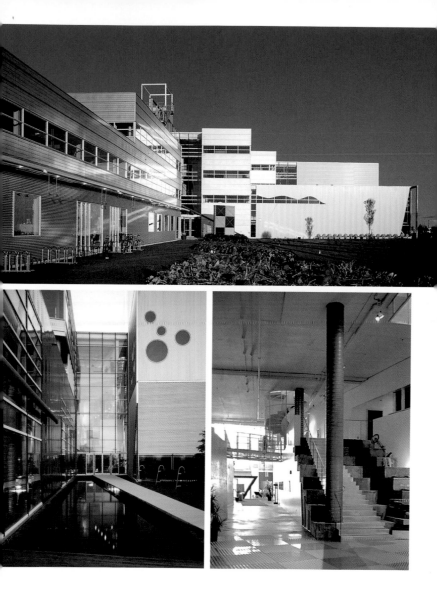

115 STUDIOS – CIRQUE DU SOLEIL

This series of studios houses artists and performers who come to train with the Cirque du Soleil before joining one of its many productions.
In reality there are two buildings: a pile of "stacked containers" that faces the Cirque du Soleil headquarters across the street, and a low three-storey block on Jean-Rivard, which is more in scale with the housing immediately to the east. The starkness of the low block, while enlivened by an alternating window pattern, is almost too modest next to the exuberance of the containers. Both volumes are clad in copper-coloured metal panels that radiate warmth.

Some studios can be combined to create larger spaces; all have access to communal areas, including a fitness room, an internet café and living rooms. The studios in the cube of containers are built around a glazed central atrium – light floods in from above.

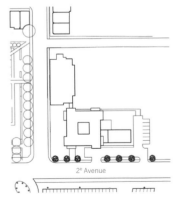

2ᵉ Avenue

Architects **FABG**
Client **Cirque du Soleil**
Completed **2004**
Address **8333 2ᵉ Avenue**
Métro **d'Iberville (+ bus 94 nord)**
Access **exterior only**

ÉCOLE NATIONALE DE CIRQUE

The École nationale de cirque sits like a tall ship becalmed in the somewhat bleak landscape of the Cité des arts du cirque. In this way, it fulfils its original purpose – as a signpost for the precinct from the Metropolitan expressway.

A well-composed object, its height is a function of the architects' decision to stack the two eleven-metre-high gymnasia required for trapeze and aerial work. Extensive glazing provides natural light for the gyms, diffused by sun shades on the sloped west face and by translucent glass on the north. Performance spaces are in the centre, while classrooms and offices are on the perimeter of the building.

The landscaped sculpture terrace at the entry designed by NIP paysage is appropriately irreverent – this is a circus school – but the semi-submerged space below looks strangely like a basement apartment.

Architects	**Lapointe Magne et Associés**
Landscape architects	**NIP paysage**
Client	**École nationale de cirque**
Completed	**2003**
Address	**8181 2ᵉ Avenue**
Métro	**d'Iberville (+ bus 94 nord)**
Access	**exterior only**

ST. MICHEL

TOHU

As the public face of the *Cité des arts du cirque,* TOHU is a performance space, a community cultural centre, and a gateway to the St. Michel Environmental Complex. The name comes from *tohu-bohu*, meaning hurly-burly or confusion – the chaos that precedes renewal. Built to be an exemplar of sustainability, TOHU is a worthy solution to a demanding programme.

The grey- and green-coloured cylindrical theatre dominates the structure. Built of pre-cast, self-load-bearing concrete panels, it is a permanent big top for circus presentations. An exhibition area and offices for the not-for-profit organization that manages TOHU occupy a low wing tangential to the circular hall. The back-of-house and artists' entrance are on the opposite, expressway, side of the theatre.

The most innovative aspects of this project are not immediately apparent, including a passive geothermic / low-velocity diffusion heating and ventilation system that reduces energy use by seventy per cent, relative to a conventional installation. Radiant in-floor heating in the concrete slabs uses water warmed by waste heat from the adjacent biogas plant. A particularly theatrical gesture in the main lobby is a glass panel inset into the floor, which allows a look at the "ice box" below – a natural cooling system.

Architects **Schème / Jacques Plante / Jodoin Lamarre Pratte et Associés**
Client **TOHU, La Cité des arts du cirque**
Completed **2004**
Address **2345 Jarry est (entry via des Regrattiers)**
Métro **d'Iberville (+ bus 94 nord)**
Access **Tuesday to Sunday / www.tohu.ca**

UNIVERSITÉ DE MONTRÉAL / OUTREMONT

Université de Montréal inaugurated its new campus on the north side of Mount Royal in 1943, having moved from the Quartier Latin, the area around St. Denis and Ste. Catherine. The site, given to the university by the City of Montreal, bordered the community of Côte-des-Neiges. Predominantly rural until the First World War, the area developed rapidly in the 1920s, in part due to the tramways and in part because of the start of construction of St. Joseph's Oratory (completed only in 1955) and other institutions such as Collège Jean-de-Brébeuf. Today Côte-des-Neiges is home to a multiplicity of hospitals and schools.

The Université de Montréal campus and its principal building are the work of renowned Montreal architect Ernest Cormier. The central pavilion is a graceful example of the monumentality that characterised the 1930s in other parts of the world – less common in Montreal because there was so little built during the Depression. Indeed, construction of the central pavilion with its now-iconic tower started in 1928 but was stopped entirely for more than ten years.

Subsequent construction from the 1960s to the 1990s has densified the campus significantly and direct links to a metro station have made it more accessible.

Outremont is an affluent, primarily residential community with generous street widths, mature trees and a network of parks established in the 1910s with the deliberate intention of maintaining its garden city character.

PAVILLON DE LA FACULTÉ DE L'AMÉNAGEMENT

In 1994, Université de Montréal mounted an architectural competition to enlarge and renovate the former convent that housed the Faculté de l'aménagement (home to architecture, landscape architecture, interior design, urban planning and industrial design), to create a new landscaped public space and integrate the whole into the fabric of the university campus. Saucier + Perrotte's winning solution positioned a rectangular volume for studios to intersect with the original building. However, the signature piece of the project is the dark red four-hundred-seat auditorium, inserted into the void created by removing the chapel from the existing building. A generous entry lobby, complete with grand staircase, functions as crush space for the auditorium and, more importantly, as part of the public life of the building.

On the Côte Ste. Catherine façade, a Cor-Ten panel was superimposed on the existing yellow brick in a curiously unsuccessful gesture devised to signal the presence of the auditorium. On the campus side, the new construction is wrapped in a grate-like curtain wall pierced by a bridge, which serves as the principal access to the building. Once inside, the bridge traverses an interior courtyard space and exhibition gallery below.

Studios in the new block were conceived and built as entirely open space, partly in the Bauhaus tradition, partly as reaction to the tightly crammed layout of the existing convent building.

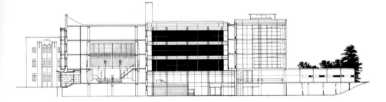

Architects	**Saucier + Perrotte / Menkès Shooner Dagenais**
Client	**Université de Montréal**
Completed	**1997**
Address	**2940 Chemin de la Côte-Sainte-Catherine**
Métro	**Université-de-Montréal**
Access	**university hours**

UNIVERSITÉ DE MONTRÉAL

HEC MONTRÉAL

Affiliated with the Université de Montréal, HEC Montréal (the École des hautes études commerciales) underwent a massive growth spurt in the early 1990s with the surge of students wanting to become part of *Québec Inc.,* as the movement to Quebec-owned and-run businesses was described. The choice of site for the business school was controversial not only because it implied destruction of some untouched woodlands on the sloping south side of Côte Ste. Catherine, but also because of the scale of the insertion into the neighbourhood. At 44,550 square metres, the building is often compared to an ocean liner berthed on the periphery of the campus.

The interior of HEC Montréal is large scale but coherent. The resolutely linear circulation draws the visitor to the centre of the building. Functions are stacked vertically: classrooms are on the first floor, the library on the second, and offices on the floors above.

At the heart of the second floor, a three-storey-high winter garden is the public space with cafeteria, gallery and meeting rooms. A surprising west wall, entirely glazed, curves into the plan as if to leave room for the trees beyond.

Natural light pours down cylindrical clerestories all the way from the seventh floor, infusing the core of the building with light.

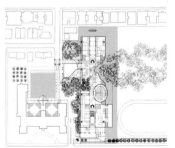

Côte Ste. Catherine

Architects	**Dan S. Hanganu / Jodoin Lamarre Pratte et Associés**
Client	**Université de Montréal**
Completed	**1996**
Address	**3000 Chemin de la Côte-Ste-Catherine**
Métro	**Université-de-Montréal**
Access	**university hours**

PAVILLON J.-ARMAND-BOMBARDIER DE L'ÉCOLE POLYTECHNIQUE

Buildings on the main campus of the Université de Montréal are required to be clad in the yellow brick used by Ernest Cormier for the iconic central pavilion in 1942. Here the north and west sides of the Bombardier pavilion face towards the central campus, their pale yellow brick alternating with horizontal bands of glazing that allow natural light into offices. Charcoal-colour brick on the south and east indicates the core block of laboratories.

The building houses an interdisciplinary group of science and engineering researchers from the École polytechnique and the Université de Montréal. Setting the offices at the perimeter and wrapping them around the laboratory block is a deceptively simple solution to a complex program that must meet the very diverse needs of seven hundred researchers.

The sobriety of the exterior belies the richness of the interior. Natural light pours through the oversized windows and a series of small lounges where people may gather to exchange ideas or eat lunch punctuates the perimeter. The orange-metal-clad atrium – five metres wide and five storeys high – is a connector and a brilliant unexpected slice of colour.

To the north and downhill from the Bombardier pavilion, the 2005 Pavillons Lassonde by Saia Barbarese Topouzanov /Desnoyers Mercure / MSDL architects are LEED gold certified buildings in which departments of the École polytechnique are located. They are noteworthy for their use of colour in the interior as a system of identification.

Architects	**Provencher Roy et Associés / Desnoyers Mercure et Associés / Menkès Shooner Dagenais**
Client	**École polytechnique**
Completed	**2004**
Address	**Chemin de Polytechnique**
Métro	**Université-de-Montréal**
Access	**university hours**

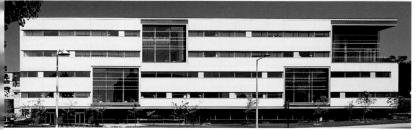

LES PROJETS EUROPA, PHASE 4

In an industrial sector of Outremont adjoining the railway tracks, a series of intriguing housing projects was built by the same developer in five successive phases over five years. The project revitalized a part of the *quartier* in a language and scale consistent with the neighbourhood. Each phase is relatively modest in size and scope and each is a variant on a different housing typology. Phase I on Querbes consists of eight townhouses and Phase II on De L'Épée is a mix of three-storey and single-storey units. The two phases back onto the same laneway, accessible via a *porte-cochère* on De L'Épée, in traditional Montreal fashion.

The most overtly industrial project is Phase 4, which reuses the two steel structures of a former laundry at the southwest corner of De L'Épée and Ducharme. Each of the two volumes that comprise the project – thirty apartments in total – fronts onto the two streets. Units at ground level have their own entrances. A central courtyard uses the remnants of the steel structure as the base for a system of bridges and balconies for the exterior circulation system that is at once adventurous and appropriate.

Architects **Boutros + Pratte**
Client **Jean-Pierre Houle**
Completed **2001**
Address **1100-1150 Av. Ducharme**
Métro **Outremont**
Access **exterior only**

Fielding

Randall

Parc de la
Confédération

Parc
Somerled

Somerled

Côte-Saint-Luc

Cumberland

Bessborough

Borden

Terrebonne

Grand

Royal

Harvard

Girouard

Parc
Benny

Monkland

Métro Villa-Maria

**Benny
Farm**

Notre-Dame-de-Grâce

Cavendish

Benny

Sherbrooke

Côte-Saint-Antoine

Parc
Notre-
Dame-
de-Grâce

de Maisonneuve

Upper-Lachine

Métro Vendôme

Saint-Jacques

Pullman

Autoroute Décarie

Décarie

Autoroute Ville-Marie

0   400 metres

4 minutes to walk

NOTRE DAME DE GRÂCE

BENNY FARM

NDG, as this borough of the City of Montreal is known, was melon farms and apple orchards until the latter part of the 19th century. A village located on Décarie between Côte St. Antoine and Notre Dame de Grâce, at the easternmost edge of present-day NDG, served the farms. Institutional presence around the original village is still very evident: many of the convents and monasteries owned by various religious orders were converted to other uses in the 1990s – principally condominiums – with very mixed results architecturally. The character of eastern NDG had, however, already been dramatically transformed by the 1967 construction of the depressed Décarie expressway.

At the turn of the 20th century, tramways provided access to and from a growing downtown. The new suburb was built almost entirely in the forty year period prior to the Second World War – a mix of semi-detached single family houses to the north, duplexes to the south and walk-up apartments along Sherbrooke, the principal commercial artery.

At the western border of NDG, Concordia University's Loyola College campus was built by the Jesuits to serve the English Catholic community in 1916. Contemporary additions to Concordia include the Richard J. Renaud Building (2003) by Marosi + Troy / Jodoin Lamarre Pratte et Associés / Cardinal Hardy.

BENNY FARM

Built in 1947 to house Second World War veterans and their families, a series of brick three-storey walk-ups was spread over two super-blocks on a 7.3-hectare site. By the early 1990s, the buildings were aging and no longer meeting the residents' needs. However, discussion about how to redevelop the site as a whole, to be appropriate in form and in use to the community – including how to reuse of some of the existing buildings – lasted more than twelve years. Community involvement in the project remained remarkably strong throughout the process, which culminated in a task force in 2002.

Four architectural firms participated in the Task Force. Saia Barbarese Topouzanov was given the mandate in 2003 to develop the site plan. Their solution provided the oversized blocks with private and semi-public spaces neatly defined by pedestrian streets; Cormier's landscape plan retained the community garden at the heart of the block.

Architects	**Saia Barbarese Topouzanov (master plan)**
Landscape architects	**Claude Cormier (master plan)**
Client	**Canada Lands Company, CMHC and others**
Completed	**1996–2007**
Address	**Rues Monkland and Sherbrooke between Walkley and Benny**
Métro	**Vendôme (+ bus 105 ouest) or Villa-Maria (+ bus 162 ouest)**
Access	**exterior only**

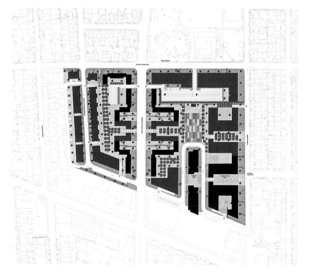

BENNY FARM

Saia Barbarese designed Les Habitations Benny Farm, an elegant apartment block for veterans, orange-brick clad with pixellated green glass-wrapped balconies. Anthracite-coloured stucco on the interior face of the two buildings defines the more private courtyard side.

Claude Cormier's landscape design for Les Habitations Benny Farm includes visually rich interior courtyards that layer hard surface and vegetation, private and public spaces.

Architects	**Saia Barbarese / Laverdière + Giguêre**
Landscape architects	**Claude Cormier**
Client	**Canada Lands Company**
Completed	**2000**
Address	**Rue Benny and 3700 and 3800 Veterans Lane**
Métro	**Vendôme (+ bus 105 ouest)**
	or Villa-Maria (+ bus 162 ouest)
Access	**exterior only**

L'OEUF, an architectural firm that had participated in the Benny Farm process from the beginning, designed Chez Soi, affordable housing for seniors on Cavendish. The glazed ground floor space of the six-storey brick building is like a front porch on the neighbourhood. Built according to sustainable principles, the building is heated by a combination of heat sources – the solar and geothermal provided by Green Energy Benny Farm, a community-based not-for-profit small energy company.

L'OEUF has been responsible for the recycling and rebuilding of three other existing buildings on Benny Farm: two housing cooperatives and housing for young mothers.

Architects **L'OEUF (Zoo and Chez Soi)**
Clients **Chez Soi**
Completed **2006**
Address **3825 Rue Cavendish**
Métro **Vendôme (+ bus 105 ouest)**
Access **exterior only**

Guy

Richmond

Saint-Martin

des Seigneurs

**Centre sportif
de la Petite-
Bourgogne**

Canning

Métro Georges-Vanier

Georges-Vanier

**Les Habitations
Georges-Vanier**

Dominion

Saint-Jacques

Lionel-Groulx

Delisle

Workman

Notre-Dame

**Canal de
Lachine**

Canal de Lachine

Autoroute Ville-Marie

Saint-Antoine

Coursol

Vinet

Duvernay

Sainte-Cunégonde

des Écluses

Saint-Patrick

Augustin-Cantin

Centre

Grand Trunk

Mullins

Charlevoix

Métro Lionel-Groulx

Atwater

Greene

Marché
Atwater

Rufus-Rockhead

Métro Charlevoix

Rose-de-Lima

**Residence
Saint-Ambroise**

**Les habitations
Saint-Ambroise**

Bourget

Sainte-Émilie

Turgeon

Saint-Augustin

Saint-Ambroise

Place
Saint-
Henri

Couvent

Métro Place-Saint-Henri

**Les Habitations
Saint-Ambroise**

Bos

Saint-Ferdinand

**Lofts
Redpath**

**Agmont
America**

0   200 metres

ST. HENRI / LACHINE CANAL / LITTLE BURGUNDY

Canada's premier industrial heritage site, the Lachine Canal was built in 1825 to link the Montreal harbour to Lac St. Louis, bypassing the Lachine Rapids and allowing navigation to penetrate the North American continent. The canal was used continuously until 1970, when the 1959 St. Lawrence Seaway became the sole route for ships.

The canal was the cradle of industry in Canada; refineries, mills and factories lined its banks in the mid-19th century as they not only used the canal to ship their goods but as a source of hydraulic power. The neighbourhoods on both sides of the canal were built up in the latter part of the 19th century as housing for those who worked in the factories. To the south of the canal Point St. Charles was dominated by railway yards, to the north St. Henri and Little Burgundy were a mix of residential and industrial. The 1965 City of Montreal urban renewal project demolished in order to rebuild much of the affordable housing in Little Burgundy.

The fourteen-kilometre-long Canal and its banks is now a linear park, owned and maintained as an historic site by Parks Canada, and restored as a navigable waterway in 2002.

Recycling of industrial structures along the canal started in the mid-1980s with the conversion of the former Stelco steel plant and the Belding-Corticelli silk mill into condominiums. Recession in the 1990s slowed conversion and new construction was almost non-existent, but from 2000 onwards condominiums have sprouted like mushrooms, particularly around the Atwater Market.

RUE SAINT-AMBROISE

Rue St. Ambroise is at the southern limit of St. Henri bordering the Lachine Canal, the site of 19th-century factories and mills. Revitalization started slowly in the early 1990s with conversion of industrial buildings for artists' studios and lofts – new construction was limited to houses built by architects for themselves.

Neatly occupying the corner, the four-level single-family house at 70 Rose-de-Lima is inserted into a tightly-constrained lot at the intersection with St. Ambroise. Its subdued, simple language and stucco cladding set it apart from the vernacular of the neighbourhood. Interiors are open-plan, organized around a central staircase.

On the east side of Rose-de-Lima, on a triangular site bought from the City of Montreal immediately opposite the Atwater Market, Les habitations St. Ambroise attracted attention from the start. Its site, its construction in the mid-1990s, when little or no construction was going on in Montreal, and its adherence to sustainable principles set it apart. Definitely not the typical linear Montreal housing type, its four units are stacked and sorted vertically. All living and sleeping spaces are housed on the first and second floors. The ground floor is reserved for studios, garages and offices.

Résidence Saint-Ambroise
70 Rue Rose-de-Lima

Les habitations Saint-Ambroise
81 Rue Rose-de-Lima

Architects **Fortin / Shoiry**
Completed **1992**
Métro **Lionel-Groulx**

Architects **l'OEUF**
Completed **1996**
Métro **Lionel-Groulx**

As living on the banks of the Lachine Canal became fashionable in the late 1990s, a series of condominiums were built in rapid succession, particularly in the stretch near the Atwater Market. The seven-unit construction at 3701 to 3711 St. Ambroise is the only one to carry on the adventurous spirit of the earlier houses on Rose-de-Lima. Each unit reads like an individual address. Materials vary from red brick to shiplapped zinc shingles, and glazing is generous. Large deck-size balconies and steel stairways take full advantage of the courtyard to the rear, best seen from Bourget.

Further west on St. Ambroise, the principal structure in the Merchants' Manufacturing complex was built in 1880 for textile production and was one of the first conversions to offices and studios in the early 1990s. A wing and a subsequent annex have been transformed for use as offices for the advertising firm Bos, by architect Luc Laporte. The box-like annex has been entirely clad in copper shingles, giving it a presence both on the canal side and from the street.

Les Habitations Saint-Ambroise
3701–3711 Rue Saint-Ambroise

Bos
3970 Rue Saint-Ambroise

Architects **Affleck + de la Riva**
Completed **2003**
Métro **Lionel-Groulx**

Architects **Luc Laporte**
Completed **2007**
Métro **Place-Saint-Henri**

LACHINE CANAL

The massive project to revitalize the canal was realized over the seven-year period from 1997 to 2004. The principal players were Parks Canada (a federal agency), the City of Montreal, and other municipalities that border the canal's length – working in concert with community and heritage groups.

The primary focus has been on encouraging recreational use in the linear park, using the traces of the industrial history as a narrative. Restoration work was extensive and included rebuilding the masonry walls and restoring the locks, which permitted the reopening of the canal as a navigable waterway in 2002.

The St. Gabriel locks at Charlevoix are the strongest vestiges of the working canal and also a node for conversion of industrial buildings. The Peel Basin at the eastern end of the Canal will ultimately be enlarged as a marina.

Contemporary intervention in this project is most evident in the area around Atwater Market. A pedestrian bridge connects the bike path on the south side of the canal to a small public square (Schème) and service pavilion by Lapointe Magne, completed in 2002.

Architects/Client	**Parks Canada / Ville de Montréal / Société du Vieux-Port de Montréal**
Completed	**2004**
Address	**14.5 km between the Old Port and Lac Saint-Louis**
Métro	**Lionel-Groulx or Charlevoix**
Access	**public**

LACHINE CANAL

LACHINE CANAL

Agmont America

This 5,100-square-metre expansion to an existing textile dye factory is eminently functional, yet goes beyond creating a big box. The rhythm of the articulated copper-coloured cladding of corrugated steel gives this project unexpected finesse. A glazed bridge connects the new construction to the original building.

Architects	**Lemay et Associés**
Client	**SODIM**
Completed	**1997**
Address	**1401 Rue Saint-Patrick**
Métro	**Charlevoix**
Access	**exterior only**

Lofts Redpath

The most significant industrial complex on the Lachine Canal, the Redpath Sugar Refinery closed in 1979 and stood derelict for twenty years. Its conversion to condominiums in three phases from 2000 to 2007 was controversial as some Montrealers would have preferred a cultural use and the intervention was subject to much scrutiny. The exoskeleton of stairways on the courtyard side is the most compelling part of the new construction. The courtyard allows access to commercial spaces at grade, including a two-storey wing fronting onto a dock.

Architects **Cardinal Hardy**
Client **Société immobilière Gueymard**
Completed **2007**
Address **1721 Rue Saint-Patrick**
Métro **Charlevoix**
Access **exterior only**

LES HABITATIONS GEORGES-VANIER

Winner of a 1991 pan-Canadian competition, *L'art de vivre en ville*, organized to seek out "original, functional and flexible designs" for families
buying a first home in the downtown area, this project takes the traditional Montreal duplex and gives it a deliberate twist. Ten units form what
is called a *tête d'îlôt*, an ensemble that terminates a block. The outside
stairways are a recognizable feature of Montreal housing, but the form
and materials set this row resolutely apart. (The grey concrete block was
originally conceived by de la Riva to be clad in stucco, evoking the 1930s,
but this was overruled by the City.) Each unit consists of a two-bedroom
apartment on the ground floor and a larger two-storey maisonette above
it. Patios at grade and roof terraces provide private outdoor space for
both residences. The path and courtyard behind are communal space.

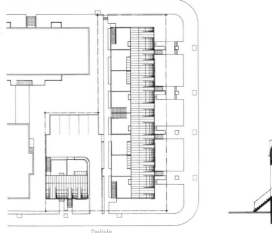

Delisle

Architects **Richard de la Riva**
Client **Ville de Montréal**
Completed **1993**
Address **corner Boul. Georges-Vanier and Av. Delisle**
Métro **Georges-Vanier**
Access **exterior only**

LITTLE BURGUNDY

CENTRE SPORTIF DE LA PETITE-BOURGOGNE

The Centre sportif de la Petite-Bourgogne is a community sports facility on an old street in a working-class neighbourhood. The building is simple, understandable, robust, and at a scale that is completely appropriate to its street-corner site. Two brick volumes – red for the gymnasium and anthracite for the swimming pool – sit on either side of an interior street. The stone-paved street follows the course of an old laneway and runs from Notre-Dame to a pedestrian path and schoolyard.

Colour and light are everywhere, and the relationship of inside to outside, particularly the pool to the park, is a delight. The simplicity of the materials is deceptive. Closer inspection reveals an attention to detail that is rare in a building constructed on a relatively modest budget.

Architects	**Saia Barbarese**
Client	**Ville de Montréal**
Completed	**1997**
Address	**1825 Rue Notre-Dame Ouest (corner of Rue des Seigneurs)**
Métro	**Georges-Vanier**
Access	**public**

Cherrier

Jacques-Bizard

Rivière des Prairies

Dupont

Lefébvre

Collège
Gérald-
Godin

Gouin Ouest

Gare Roxboro

Paiement

Laniel

Dieppe

Neveu

Saint-Pierre

Pierrefonds

Gratton

Sainte-Croix

Harry-Worth

0   200 metres
           2 minutes to walk

STE. GENEVIÈVE

COLLÈGE GÉRALD-GODIN

A tiny community on the "back river" as an earlier generation of Montrealers called the Rivière des Prairies, Ste. Geneviève still gives the visitor a strong sense of what a village in rural Quebec looked like in the mid-19th century. The parish church was built in 1843, the presbytery in 1891. The village remained fundamentally intact, as there was no direct link to downtown Montreal – the nearest train station is at Roxboro, more than ten kilometres away. However, the quietness and the proximity of the village did attract Montrealers to build summer cottages there, particularly in the first half of the 20th century.

The wave of suburbanization that washed over the western half of the island in the 1950s affected Ste. Genevieve as well: new streets were opened up and land subdivided. Construction of developer-built subdivisions continues to this day with a veritable rash of condominiums.

COLLÈGE GÉRALD-GODIN

There is a significant stock of disused religious buildings in Quebec – prime candidates for reuse. Sited on the height of land sloping down to Rivière des Prairies, the 1933 Lombard-style stone Monastère des Pères de Sainte-Croix lent itself readily to construction of a Cégep (post-secondary college) to serve the French-speaking population of Montreal's West Island.

Matching the volume of the existing building, the new construction is a black anodized aluminum-clad block that tilts as it emerges, rock-like, from the landscape. A cafeteria is semi-submerged at the base of the new wing; classrooms and laboratories are linked by a three-storey-high bridge to the older structure. A 350-seat theatre and gymnasium are below grade on a north-south axis, reaching towards the river and creating an open-air amphitheatre.

The existing monastery building is U-shaped in plan around a central courtyard. Spaces within it have been both exposed and overlaid; vaulted drywall ceilings in the corridors echo the originals. The library in the former chapel, with its internal spiral stair, is a self-contained entity – an idea that recurs in the library of Saucier + Perrotte's Schulich School of Music.

The theatricality that is Saucier + Perrotte's hallmark is given wide rein here. The visitor has a sense of the surreal, as this modernist gesture rises out of a village landscape that still evokes mid-19th-century Montreal.

Architects	**Saucier + Perrotte / Desnoyers Mercure et Associés**
Client	**Collège Gérald-Godin**
Completed	**2000**
Address	**15615 Boul. Gouin Ouest, Ste. Geneviève**
Métro	**none – train from Central Station to Roxboro (+ bus 68 ouest)**
Access	**college hours**

STE. GENEVIÈVE

AND NEXT?
RICARDO L. CASTRO

What experience and history teach is this – that people and governments never have learned anything from history, or acted on principles deduced from it.
G. W. F. Hegel, Introduction to *Philosophy of History* (1832)

The only lesson that history can teach is that history does not teach any lessons.
E. H. Carr, *What is History?* (1961)

All history is contemporary history
Benedetto Croce, *History as the Story of Liberty* (1941)

Having being invited to write a coda to this guidebook, I feel placed in the position of an oracle, a Delphian Pythia or a Roman Augur, as it were. Unfortunately, I am not trained in any of these ancient and anachronistic professions of divination. Furthermore, following Hegel and Carr's precepts about history, it would seem utterly foolish and meaningless to venture into any sort of prediction.

What I propose to do instead is to attempt a reading of certain common traits that might inform the practice of architecture in Montreal in the future, traits which begin to emerge as one experiences the various projects which the authors have chosen for the guidebook.

Design strategies present in the buildings and urban places represented and discussed in the book reinforce, in various guises, some of the environmental and architectural qualities that seem necessary to facilitate the development of Montreal into a 21st century metropolis. These qualities may be summarized as topographical engagement, transparency, the revalorization of urban space, and tectonic exploration.

Topographical engagement: Ancestral themes in which architecture occupies a symbiotic relationship with its surrounding landscape and topography – the ancient Greek theatre, the borrowed views or *Shak-kei* in Japanese gardens, and the gardens of the Baroque era are just a few examples – have resurfaced in architectural practice during the period covered by this guidebook. They resonate in several of the places illustrated. Consider the Pavillon du Jardin des Premières-Nations located in the Botanical Garden or, at a more urban level, the Centre CDP Capital. In both cases, at different scales the immediate and intermediate surroundings have become definitive assets in the internal experience of the buildings.

Transparency: This quality appears as a major criterion of the design of many of the projects in the guidebook. It does not limit itself to the simple visual experience but extends to the "synaesthetic" experience, using as many of our senses as possible. The geodesic dome originally designed by Buckminster Fuller for Expo 67 and remodelled in 1992-95 by Éric Gauthier as the Biosphere concretizes and exemplifies the idea of a monumental transparent building. It is simultaneously conceptual and physical – both in its initial execution and design and in its subsequent redesign and transformation into Environment Canada's centre for interpretation of the St. Lawrence River ecosystem. The Biosphere is a technological phoenix: it has travelled through time, adapted itself to catastrophe and emerged from the ashes.

Revalorization of urban space: Several of the projects in the guidebook engage in a definite search to create new urban places. Place D'Youville in Old Montreal, Tomlinson Square at McGill University or the Quartier international de Montréal illustrate, at different scales, a preoccupation with the introduction of new experiential values into the urban space. The architects of these projects have successfully combined "the architecture we walk on," exciting textures, urban furniture, and plant materials in an effort to differentiate and recuperate public spaces. These once undifferentiated spaces have, through their intervention, become true places.

Tectonic exploration: The construction of Maison Alcan in 1983, the erection of the Canadian Centre for Architecture and its Garden in 1989, and more recently, the renovation of the Darling Foundry and the completion of the McGill University Schulich School of Music exemplify successful, controlled explorations and expressions of the materiality of a building. This tectonic exploration often underscores the presence of the building and its integration into the urban texture; in others, it supports the sense of transparency. Think also of the Montreal Museum of Archaeology and History at Pointe-à-Callière, or the Maison Coloniale; there are, of course, many more examples in the list.

I have always believed that architecture is the remodelling of existing circumstances. Undoubtedly, to consider what our next steps will be in any direction, we have to consider where we are and where we have been – the timeless truth of Hegel and Carr notwithstanding. At a conceptual level – even historically speaking – a momentary fixation in the present is the one that colours and stimulates the next move. It is here that the Italian philosopher of history Benedetto Croce's dictum "All history is contemporary history" acquires its full meaning.

To return to the question at the beginning, *And next?* Judging by the buildings, places, landscapes and topographies assembled in *A Guidebook to Contemporary Architecture in Montreal*, I cannot but express a total sense of optimism about things to come. It is the optimism and pleasure that is derived from experiencing a significant body of work built during the past twenty-five years – it is open for exploration.

INDEX BY BUILDING / PUBLIC SPACE

INDEX BY ARCHITECT

INDEX BY BUILDING TYPE

CREDITS

All architectural drawings are reproduced courtesy of the architects with the exception of:

Maison Coloniale which is included with the kind permission of the Canadian Centre for Architecture (Fonds Jacques Rousseau), Montreal.

Canadian Centre for Architecture which is included courtesy of Canadian Centre for Architecture © Peter Rose 1989, Melvin Charney 1989

Unless otherwise indicated, the photographs were created by the architects themselves or commissioned by each firm. We have made every effort to locate and list the copyright for all illustrations. Where the credit is not listed, it is either held by the architect or we have been unable to determine the copyright holder, in which case we would ask that person to contact the publisher.

Photographers' credits:

Marie-Christine Abel, 69
Tom Arban, 34, 35 bottom right, 42, 43
© BAnQ, Bernard Fougères, 125 bottom left
Louis Bellefleur, 41, 51 top
Michel Boulet © Canadian Centre for Architecture, 31 top
Michel Brunelle, 49, 51 bottom, 71, 115, 119, 121, 143, 146, 147, 155 bottom, 172
Canadian Centre for Architecture, © Paul Labelle, 129 top and bottom right
Canadian Centre for Architecture, © Richard Pare 1989, 31 bottom left
Marc Cramer, 35 top, 53 bottom right, 61, 75, 78, 108, 109, 156, 157, 181
Roderick Chen, 87
Pierre Desjardins, 101, 136, 137
James Dow, 125 top and bottom right
Robert Etcheverry Enr., 80, 88, 89, 159, 169 left
Denis Farley, 91, 92, 94, 164
Wayne Fujii, 37
Alain Laforest, 35 bottom left, 36, 53 top, 53 bottom left, 56, 57, 59, 60, 63, 64, 65, 73, 74, 77, 79, 81, 93, 97, 112, 113, 123 top, 130 right, 131 centre and right, 132, 133 top, 149, 168, 169 right, 171, 177
Alain Laforest © Canadian Centre for Architecture, 31 bottom right, 33
Yves Lefebvre, 138, 139
Jean-François Lenoir, 175
Matt Makauskas, 162, 163
Jean Mercier, 44, 45, 47
Brian Merrett, MMFA, 28, 29
Steve Montpetit, 106, 107, 144, 145
Éric Piché, 123 bottom left and right, 153
Richard Poissant, 155 top
Fiona Spalding-Smith, 27
Michel Tremblay, 135
Jean-François Vézina, 85
Victorio Vieira, 173